The book enlightens us about various gods & goddesses of India such as Ganesha, Brahma, Vishnu, Shiva, Rama, Krishna, Narasimha, Male Deities, Female Deities and Animal Deities. Their course and career has been narrated along with their physical description.

It attempts to explain the peculiar attributes of certain gods and the reasons behind it without indulging in philosophical discourses.

Diamond Pocket Books Presents

Religion, Spirituality & Sai Literature

Mahabharata	Dr. B. R. Kishore	60.00
Ramayana	Dr. B. R. Kishore	60.00
Rigveda	Dr. B. R. Kishore	60.00
Samveda	Dr. B. R. Kishore	60.00
Yajurveda	Dr. B. R. Kishore	60.00
Atharvveda	Dr. B. R. Kishore	60.00
Hinduism	Dr. B. R. Kishore	95.00
Hindu Traditions & Beliefs (A Scientific Validity)	Dr. Bhojraj Dwivedi	150.00
Hindu Mythology and Religion (Quiz Book)	Ed. Sachin Singhal	95.00
Gods & Goddesses of India	B. K. Chaturvedi	60.00
Supreme Mother Durga (Durga Chalisa) Roman	B. K. Chaturvedi	95.00
The Hymns & Orisons of Lord Shiva (Roman)	B. K. Chaturvedi	25.00
Sri Hanuman Chalisa (Roman)	B. K. Chaturvedi	30.00
Pilgrimage Centres of India	B. K. Chaturvedi	95.00
Fast & Festivals of India	Manish Verma	50.00
Chalisa Sangrah (Roman)	R. P. Hingorani	25.00
Srimad Bhagwath Geeta (Sanskrit & English)	Dayanand Verma	50.00
Sri-Ram-Charit Manas	Ed. S. P. Ojha	120.00
Realm of Sadhana (What Saints & Masters Say)	Chakor Ajaonkar	30.00
The Spiritual Philosophy of Shri Shirdi Sai Baba Shirdi	B. Umamashwara Rao	150.00
The Immortal Fakir of Shirdi	S. P. Ruhela (Com. & Ed.)	150.00
Sai Grace and Recents Predictions	Dr. S. P. Ruhela	80.00
The Divine Glory of Shri Shirdi Sai Baba	Dr. S. P. Ruhela	150.00
Shirdi Sai : The Supreme	Dr. S. P. Ruhela	80.00
Divine Grace of Sri Shirdi Sai Baba	Dr. S. P. Ruhela	150.00
Divine Revelations of a Sai Devotee	Dr. S. P. Ruhela	50.00
The Divine Glory of Sri Shirdi Sai Baba	Chakor Ajgaonkar	40.00
Communication from the spirit of Shri Shirdi Sai Baba	Dr. S. P. Ruhela	40.00
The Footprints of Shirdi Sai	Chakor Ajgaonkar	100.00
Tales from Sai Baba's Life	Chakor Ajgaonkar	60.00
Sri Shirdi Sai Baba	B. Umamaheswara Rao	60.00
Thus Spake Sri Shirdi Sai Baba	U. Umamaheswara Rao	40.00
Sai Baba of Shirdi	B. K. Chaturvedi	60.00
Sri Sathya Sai Baba : A Biography	B. K. Chaturvedi	25.00
The Eternal Sai	B. Maaney	40.00
Sri Shirdi Sai Bhjanavali (In Roman)	Dr. S. P. Ruhela	30.00
Worship of Sri Sathya Sai Baba (In Roman)	Dr. S. P. Ruhela	90.00
His Mystery and Experiencing His Love	Dr. S. P. Ruhela	60.00
World Peace and Sri Sathya Sai Avtar	Dr. S. P. Ruhela	60.00
How to Receive Sri Sathya Sai Baba's Grace	Dr. S. P. Ruhela	100.00
The Miracle Man : Sri Sathya Sai Baba	B. K. Chaturvedi	60.00
Sri Sathya Sai Baba : Understanding Rishi Ram Ram	Yogi M. K. Spencer	100.00
Oneness with God	Yogi M. K. Spencer	90.00
Quiet Talks with the Master	Eva Bell Barber	60.00
Adventures with Evil Spirits	Joseph J. Ghosh	80.00
A Child from the Spirit world Speaks	K. H. Nagrani	10.00
Future is in Our Hand	A. Somasundaram	90.00
Fragrant Spiritual Memories of A karma Yogi	Dr. S. P. Ruhela	100.00

GODS AND GODDESSES OF INDIA

Kailash Nath Seth
B. K. Chaturvedi

Diamond Pocket Books

ISBN 81-7182-069-7

Publisher : **Diamond Publications**
X-30, Okhla Industrial Area,
Phase-II, New Delhi-110020
Phone: 011-6841033, 6822803, 6822804
Fax : 011-6925020
: mverma@nde.vsnl.net.in
: www.diamondpocketbook.com
: 2003
: Rs. 150/-
: Adarsh Printer, Naveen Shahdra, Delhi-32

Contents

INTRODUCTION

The Hindu population spread throughout the vast land of India has a common basis of religious faith, which furnishes a good evidence of the original unity of the Aryan inhabitants of this country during pre-historical days. Hinduism is like a big fig-tree growing from a single stem and then sending out numerous branches destined to strike roots to the ground and themselves becoming big trees in their own right. Thus a simple pantheistic doctrine has spread out into a vast polytheistic system with innumerable gods and goddesses and voluminous mythological literature.

Popular Hinduism believes in one Universal Being-Brahm or Omkar, that adopts so many appearances-each one having a distinctive character or displaying in part one or more attribute of the Almighty, and this provides the basis of polytheism and the pantheon on gods and goddesses. 'Three' is a sacred number constantly appearing in Hindu religious system. Agni, Indra and Surya constitute the Vedic triad of gods. There are frequent allusions in Vedas to thirty-three gods, which again is a multiple of three. Although Trimurti is not named as such in the Vedic hymns, yet Veda is the basic source of this Triad of godly personification. Vedic poet-seers had the tendency to group all the forces and energies of nature under three heads and the proliferation of the number of gods into thirty-three was the assertion that each of the leading personifications was capable of eleven transformations. The trinity of Brahma, Vishnu and Shiva holding the biggest sway in Hindu mythology today has its seed and also root in the Vedas.

In the well-known hymn of the Rig Veda elucidating the mystery of creation, we perceive the first enunciation in the world's religious literature, the idea that the Creator willed to create the universe through the agency of a female principle. This idea is expressed in the marriage of heaven and earth. The Sankhya Philosophy also expresses this idea where the union of Purush and Prakriti is mentioned. It gathered so great a strength that now every principal deity of Hindu mythology has a female companion, who shares the worship paid to the male god, e.g., Sita and Rama, Parvati and Shiva, Radha and Krishna, Lakshmi and Vishnu.

As mentioned earlier today Hindu religion is a huge structure which has spread over to an immense surface by continuous additions and accretions. All creeds and cults have found in it a refuge and home. It has even accepted Buddha as an incarnation of Vishnu. Universal tolerance and receptivity is the hallmark of Hinduism. The preference of one group to the worship of god Shiva may be termed Shaivism, while the tilt, in favour of god Vishnu may be called Vaishnavism but these are never considered as opposite or incompatible creeds. Both accept and acquiesce to a certain extent, each others' views while laying an exaggerated veneration to one distinct deity like Rama, Krishna, Shiva, Ganesha. Other gods are put together and devotees pay equal homage to all.

Incarnation of God on earth is an important facet of Hindu faith. The view holds that God descends from His abode to earth in order to eradicate evil and sins, whenever they start prevailing upon virtue and good deeds. Vishnu is the only member of the Trimurti who is able to take human form in flesh and blood for the salvation of the world in times of peril and calamity. Certainly there are references of various gods adopting human or animal form in Puranas, but the term Avatara (reincarnation) in its proper connotation is considered to be the descent of Lord Vishnu on earth. For example, there is a form of Shiva called Virabhadra (according to a few he is Shiva's son). He is depicted as fierce with a thousand heads, eyes and feet. There are also eight Bhairavas who are all various forms of Shiva. Still they are not called Avatara.

The doctrine of Bhakti (personal devotion and surrender), which though existent in small measure earlier, found a more enhanced role in the epic age. Vaishnavas enjoin their followers complete devotion to Rama or Krishna, Shaivites ask for full surrender to Shiva while Shaktas call for the same attitude towards Durga and Ganpatyas claim the same supreme status for Ganesha.

The practice of idol worship, paying homage to gods, goddesses and minor deities is today an inseparable part of Hindu religious system. There is not even one country in the world which can claim to have so many temples and shrines dedicated to gods and goddesses under different forms, images, symbols and names. The temples of the first category found in the greatest number are those of the principal gods, namely Shiva and Parvati, seen in almost all temples. In the South, the shrines of the other son of Shiva, named Karttikeya are commonly found. Secondly the shrines dedicated to monkey-god Hanuman and to the terrible form of the Parvati, namely Durga are found all over India. In some cities like Varanasi besides the important shrines, a few temples of Navgrahas (the nine planets), symbolised as nine gods, are also found. They are generally being conciliated before marriage ceremony and few other auspicious family functions.

Though carved images of some gods like Indra, Varuna, Kuvera, Kama, Parsuram, Yama and Varaha are scattered in the land here and there, shrines dedicated exclusively to them are seldom found. Same is the case with animal gods like Garuda, Sheshanaga and the cow Annapurna.

Idols in temples of towns and cities are not the only images worshipped by Hindus. In the smallest of villages and the most neglected localities, at the top of hills, on raised plateaus and below stately trees one can see, if not an unfinished or dilapidated temple, but at least rough idols or simple blocks of some local god or deity consecrated by putting sindoor (red paint) over it.

Out of hundreds of Hindu gods and goddesses a few have been included here. Their course and career has been narrated along with their physical description. This book attempts to explain the peculiar attributes of certain gods and the reasons behind it without indulging in philosophical discourses. The treatment is neither exhaustive nor scholarly. It is meant to satisfy a layman's curiosity concerning chief deities, whom one comes across most frequently while visiting places in this ancient land, known as Bharatavarsha, Aryavarta, Jambudvipa, Hindustan or India.

Lord Shri Ganeshji

Lord Ganesh — considered as first amongst gods and being the remover of obstacles and is also known as Vighneshvara.

GANESHA

Ganesha, popularly known and easily recognised as the Elephant-God, is one of the most important deities of the Hindu pantheon. Before every undertaking, be it laying of the foundation of a house, or opening of a shop or beginning any other work, Lord Ganesha is first worshipped so as to invoke his blessings.

Ganesha has many names. The main ones are Ganapati (lord of the tribe or attendants), Vighneshvara (controller of all obstacles), Vinayaka (the prominent leader), Gajaanana (elephant-faced), Gajadhipati (Lord of elephants), Lambkarna (long-eared), Lambodara (pendant-bellied) and Ekadanta (having one tusk).

Ganesha is the son of Lord Shiva and goddess Parvati (Shiva's consort). The story connected with his birth and having an elephant's head is an interesting episode in the Hindu mythology. On one occasion when Parvati was going to take her bath, she, for reasons of privacy and protection, created Ganesha from her sweat and scurf and asked him to guard her apartments. Shiva, who returned from his journey, sought admission into the house. Ganesha unaware of his identity refused the entry. Shiva was enraged and he cut off Ganesha's head. Hearing the scuffle Parvati appeared and tearfully explained that the victim was their offspring. On hearing the sad news Shiva ordered his attendants to look around and bring back the head of a child whose mother might be sleeping with her back towards it. Only one mother-elephant was found sleeping in this posture and the severed head of this cub-elephant was brought to Shiva and he fixed this head onto his son's shoulders.

There is another legend accounting for Ganesha's elephant-head. One day Parvati, proud of the handsome face of her son, asked Shani (Saturn) to have a look at the child. She completely forgot about the disastrous effects of Shani's glance and when Shani looked, the child's visage burnt to ashes. Brahma (the creator of the universe) advised Parvati in distress to replace the head with the first she could find and the child would come to life. The first one to be found was that of an elephant, and this way Ganesha acquired the head of an elephant.

Another myth is that once Shiva slew Aditya, the son of a sage, (though later restored him to life again) outraged at this, Kashyapa, one of the seven great Rishis, doomed that Shiva's son will also lose his head. When the curse actually got realised, the head of Indra's elephant replaced it. Still another version states that on one occasion after Parvati had bathed, the water was thrown into the Ganges and drunk by the elephant-headed goddess Malini who gave birth to a baby with four arms and five elephant heads. The river-goddess Ganga claimed him, but Shiva declared him to be the son of Parvati, combined the five heads into a single one and enthroned him as the 'Remover of obstacles' (Vighneshvara).

The mythical explanations of Ganesha's solitary tusk (Ekadanta) also makes an interesting study. The most popular legend represents that Parsuram (another incarnation of God with an axe as his weapon) once came to Mount Kailash, the abode of Shiva, the father of Ganesha. He was on a friendly visit to Shiva, who was in deep sleep at that time. Ganesha opposed the entrance of the visitor to the inner apartments. A hotworded wrangle ensued, which culminated in a fight. Initially Ganesha had the advantage in the duel. He seized Parsuram with his trunk and gave him a swift twirl, which left him sick and senseless.

After recovering, Parsuram threw his axe at Ganesha. Shiva had given this axe to Parsuram as a gift, Ganesha recognised his own father's weapon, and received it with all humility on one of his tusks, which immediately got severed off. Since then Ganesha has one tusk and is known as the single-tusked. The other story is that on one occasion, the moon and the twenty-seven asterisms (nakshatras) laughed at Ganesha's pot belly. In great rage he broke off one of his tusks and threw it at the moon which gradually became dark due to the wound.

Ganesha is depicted as having four arms which symbolise him as the universal ruler, establishing his power over the four categories of beings, viz., firstly those who can live only in water, secondly those who can live in water and earth, thirdly those who can live only on earth and lastly those who can fly in the air. Moreover it was god Ganesha, who instituted the four castes and the four Vedas. One hymn in Sri Bhagavat Tattva, an ancient scripture, says: 'In heaven this child will establish the predominance over gods, on earth that of men, in the nether world that of the anti-gods and serpents. He causes the four principles of the elements to move and is therefore four armed. In one hand he is shown to be holding a shell, in another a discus, in the third a club or a sweet cake and in the fourth a water lily.'

The vehicle of Ganesha is a mouse. As rats generally succeed in gnawing their way through every obstruction, the rat symbolises this god's ability to destroy every obstacle. Being an elephant he passes through the thickest of wild growth in a forest, uproots and tears the thickest trees hindering his path and fells out whatever comes in his way. In the same way like a mouse he also can slip through the narrowest of spaces and thickest of the walls by drilling holes. Moreover a mouse is deemed to be the master of everything inside. The all-pervading Atman (soul) is the mouse that lives in the hole called Intellect, within the heart of every being. It hides itself behind the inscrutable shape of illusion.

The legend about Ganesha having preference over all other gods establishes his sharpness of intellect. There was a keen competition amongst all gods to gain the first place of worship amongst the laity. It was decided that the god, who will return first after traversing the whole universe shall be declared the winner. All god and goddesses ran on their fast vehicles. Ganesha with his pot-bellied body and mouse as vehicle could never hope to compete. He took a round of his parents, Shiva and Parvati, and just sat there at the starting point. He was declared the winner because one who goes round his parents and touches their feet traverses the whole universe. Since then Ganesha is always worshipped first and every other god takes a back seat. Another legend says that when Parvati saw an elephant's head being fixed on her son's body, she burst into tears and could not be soothed. To pacify her Brahma announced that Ganesha will get precedence over other gods in the matter of worship.

Ganesha has got two wives, one named Siddhi (Success) and the other named Ridhi (Prosperity). One who pleases the Lord, automatically comes in the good books of his two wives. Ganesha, the embodiment of wisdom, is also depicted as a scribe to whom sage Vyasa dictated the Mahabharata. He is accepted as the god of learning and the patron of letters.

In modern age Ganesha is regarded as the personification of those qualities which surmount all difficulties. He is the typical lord of success in life and its accompaniments like good living, prosperity and peace. Not only is Ganesha thus honoured in religious ceremonies, but in almost all civil concerns too his blessings are sought. For example, on the head of letters, in opening pages of account books, at the entrance gate of house and at the door of a shop, salutation to Ganesha by depicting his image or his symbol is deemed to be auspicious and a guarantee for progress and prosperity. His numerous images and shrines can be seen throughout India. In all ceremonies (except funeral rites) Ganesha is first invoked. He is revered by most Hindus, whether followers of Shiva or Vishnu.

Ganesha was born on the fourth day of the month of Bhadrapad or Bhadon, the sixth month of the Hindu lunar calendar. Although worship of Ganesha is widespread all over India, in south and in Maharashtra the people are particularly attached to this god. The main features of the festivities are the buying or making of a clay image of Ganesha, worshipping the idol at home or a community centre and then taking it in a procession to be immersed in a river, lake or sea. The image is taken in a palanquin or on head.

Ganesha represents the unity of the small being, the man, with the great being, the elephant. It is the blending of the microcosm with the macrocosm, of a drop with the ocean and of an individual soul with the divinty.

OM

Om is the most sacred syllable, the first sound of the Almighty- the sound from which emerges each and every other sound, whether of music or of language. In the Upanishads this sacred syllable appears as a mystic sound, regarded by scriptures as the very basis of every other sacred mantra (hymn). It is the sound not only of origination but also of dissolution. The past, present and future are all included in this one sound and even all that transcends this configuration of time is also implied in OM.

According to Taittriya Upanishad the origin of language is assigned to Prajapati, from whose meditation on the three words arose the three Vedas and from his meditation, arose the three syllables, bhoor, bhuva and svaha, which represents earth, atmosphere and the sky. From his meditation on these three originated the divine syllable of OM, which coordinated all speech and represents the Trimurti (triad) of Brahma, Vishnu and Shiva.

Shiva's drum produced this sound and through it came the notes of the octave, i.e., Sa, Ri, Ga, Ma, Pa, Dha, Ni, Sa. Thus by this sound Shiva creates and recreates the universe. OM is also the sound form of Atman.

The Upanishads state that everything, existent and non-existent, can be grasped by uttering the sacred syllable of OM. The psycho-therapic efficacy of OM is deemed limitless and its utterance redeems all errors in the performance of a sacrifice. Meditation on OM satisfies every need and ultimately leads to liberation. Nearly all the prayers and recital of sacred passages are prefixed by the utterance of OM. Its equivalent is Omkara, venerated in the same manner and is thought to be the representation of God Himself.

Musically, it is also held that the OM or AUM is made up by three base notes 'A' 'U' 'M' or the basic 'Sa' 'Pa' of the fundamental scale and again Sa (the base note) of the immediately higher scale. When one pronounces these notes in continuity, all the basic notes from Sa to Ni also resound. Similarly when one pronounces AUM correctly, all the basic sounds also echo. It is believed to be the traditional way of clearing up all the impediments in the vocal chord to make one chant the hymns correctly. Their unison makes one not only sound sonorous but also acts as the necessary preparation to chant a Mantra (Incantation) correctly. It is for this reason that all the Vedic Mantras has 'OM' or 'AUM' as the first term.

Lord Brahma

Lord Brahma — the Creator, associated with the creation of the universe and the first god of the Hindu triad.

Lord Brahma — the Creator, associated with the creation of the

BRAHMA

Brahma, the first member of the Hindu trinity though much less important than the other two, namely Vishnu and Mahesha, is manifested as the active creator of this universe. The name Brahma is not found in the Vedas and the Brahmanas, where the active creator is merely known as Golden-embryo (Hirayna-garbha) or the Lord of Progeny (Praja-pati). The Mahabharata considers him as born from the embryo which took shape in Vishnu's mind when he began to think of creation.

After the destruction of one universe Vishnu falls asleep, floating on the causal waters. When another universe is to be created, Brahma appears on a lotus, which springs from the navel of Vishnu. Hence Brahma is also called Navel-born (Nabhi-ja) or the Lotus-born (Kinja-ja). When Brahma creates the world it remains in existence for one of his days, which means 2,160,000,000 years in terms of Hindu calendar. When Brahma goes to sleep after the end of his day, the world and all that is therein is consumed by fire. When he awakes he again restores the whole creation. This goes on till the hundred years of Brahma's life is completed. When this period ends he himself loses his existence, and he and all gods and sages, and the whole universe are dissolved into their constituent elements.

Brahma is shown as having four heads though originally he had five. The acquirement of five heads and the subsequent loss of one head makes an interesting legend. According to myths, he originally possessed only one head. After cutting a part of his own body Brahma created a woman Shatarupa (a face with hundred beauties). She is also called Vach or Sarasvati, Savitri, the solar hymn, Gayatri, the triple hymn and Sandhya (twilight). As soon as Brahma saw his female creation, he fell in love with her and could not remove his eyes from her extraordinary beauty. Naturally, Shatarupa felt shy and tried to evade his gaze by moving away on all sides. To follow her wherever she moved, Brahma created more heads-one on the left, second on the right and the third at the back of the original first. Shatarupa then rose towards the sky to escape his gaze and Brahma created the fifth head on top of all the four. This way he came to have five heads.

It is mentioned in the scriptures that the fifth head was chopped off by Shiva. He spoke most disrespectfully about Shiva, who in his anger opened the fiery third eye which burnt off his fifth head.

Brahma has four arms and he holds a lotus flower, his sceptre, his bow parivita, a string of beads, a bowl containing the holy water and the Vedas. He is therefore also called Chaturanana or Chaturmukha (four-faced) and Ashta-Karna (eight-eared). He is usually shown as a bearded man in the full maturity of age. According to Shiva Purana, from the incestual union of Brahma and Shatarupa was born Svayambhuva Manu, the progenitor of man, and from him in turn all creatures.

Brahma's vehicle is the swan or goose, the symbol of knowledge. He is therefore said to be riding on the swan (Hansa-vahana). He is the source of all knowledge and his consort, Sarasvati, is the goddess of knowledge. Brahma was the father of Daksha, who is said to have sprung from his thumb and Brahma personally was present at the sacrificial ceremony of that king, which was badly disturbed by Rudra. The four Kumars, the chief of whom was called Sanat Kumar, were also the sons of Brahma, who were born later. He is also the creator of beautiful Ahalya, whom he married off to sage Gautama. She is the same Ahalya, who became a rock piece as a result of a curse by her husband because she was seduced by Indra, the king of heavenly spirits. She was brought to her natural human form when Lord Rama touched the rock by his feet. After this she was reconciled to her husband.

Today though Brahma's name is invoked in many religious services, his image is worshipped nowhere except at Pushkara temple, near Ajmer. Brahma seems to have been thrown into shade probably because in Hindu mind he has ceased to function actively after creation of the world, though he will exert himself again while creating a new universe when this present one will meet its end. In fact his dynamic powers of creation have now been arrogated by Vishnu and Shiva, who appeal much more to popular imagination. Understandably, the legends about this god are not so numerous or rich as those centred round the other two of the triad.

One very plausible reason for Brahma (the Creator), becoming rather unpopular among the devotees is because of his being rather callous in granting boons to the demons unguardedly. It is more than a coincidence that all the deadly demons, right from Hiranyakashipu to Ravana received their boons from Brahma which made them singularly notorious in damaging the noble virtues of the world. Then it became necessary for Lord Vishnu to appear in his various incarnations to kill these demons. That is why the cult of Brahma's worship declined. The Hindus, later on, began to deem Brahma as the sole god of worship for the demons. Hence everywhere in India, there are uncountable temples to worship Lord Vishnu and Lord Shiva while the third companion in the Triumvirate, Lord Brahma has only one temple which is at the Pushkar Lake in Ajmer.

There is another primeval being associated with Brahma called Viraj or 'ruling' who dwells in paradise. Certain legends consider Viraj as his son whereas some others consider Viraj as his daughter. One myth accounts that once Brahma in the form of Apava (water mover), divided himself into two : the primeval male, Purusha; and the primeval female Viraj. But some other myths hold the view that Purusha and Viraj emerged from one another. And from the union of Brahma and

Viraj, Svayambhuva Manu was born. It is held that Viraj is the other name of Shatarupa and also known as Prakriti personifying nature, or the female sex and Maya or illusion. Brahma (masculine) the god is different from Brahm (neuter), the supreme soul. Brahm means the Absolute or the Ultimate Principle.

Lord Vishnuji

Lord Vishnu — the Preserver sometimes represented as dark complexioned usually holds in his four hands a Padma (lotus), a Gada (mace), a Shanka (conch), and a Chakra (discus).

VISHNU

Hindu gods and goddesses are phenomenal, but in due course of time Vishnu, as God of all gods, acquired supremacy, which continues till date. He is the central and the major diety of the trinity, viz., Brahma, Vishnu and Shiva. Though technically amongst these three chief gods known as the Creator, the Preserver, and the Destroyer, Vishnu is the Preserver and for all practical purpose he is deemed to be omnipotent, omnipresent and omniscient.

The name Vishnu comes from the root vish, which means "to spread in all directions," "to pervade". Hence Vishnu is the Pervader. He is the inner centre, the core, the nucleus, the cohesive point through which everything exists. He swells in everything, owns everything and overcomes anything. According to scriptures, old and not so old, Vishnu is known by innumerable names. Shankaracharya's commentary on the Vishnu-Sahasra-nama explains the meaning of a thousand names of Vishnu.

At the dawn of Aryan religion's formative stage, Vishnu is found to be a god amongst so many other gods. But his rise on the scale of worship and prayer occurred very rapidly and already before the end of the Vedic times, he rises to the highest pedestal. The form and image of Vishnu as well as its significance is explained in detail in Puranas and several other minor Upanishads. The two most common representations of Vishnu show him either sleeping over the waves of the ocean on the coils of the serpent-deity, named Sheshanaga, or standing on waves with four hands-each hand holding one of his four chief attributes.

Gopal-uttartapani Upanishad gives an explicit description of the four arms of Vishnu. "In my lower right hand, which represents the revolving or creative tendency, I hold the conch, symbol of the five elements... In the upper right hand, which represents the cohesive tendency, I hold the discus, shining like an infant sun, symbol of the mind... In the upper left hand which represents the tendency towards dispersion and liberation, I hold the lotus, symbol of the causal power of illusion, from which the universe rises... In my lower left hand, which represents the notion of individual existence, is the mace, symbol of primeval knowledge."

The Conch (Shankh) named Panchjanya is the fountain that evolves the five elements, i.e., water, fire, air, earth and sky or space. When blown, it produces a sound that is associated with the primeval sound from which creation developed. The Discus or wheel (Chakra) of Vishnu named Sudershana has six spokes and symbolises six-petalled lotus. It represents the limitless controlling of all the six seasons and is the fearful weapon that severs the head of demons. The Lotus of Vishnu is named Padma. It is the symbol of purity and represents the unfolding of creation. It is the truth (Sathva), the element from which emerged the rules of conduct (Dharma) and knowledge (Jnana). The Mace (Gada) of Vishnu is named Kaumodaki which represents the elemental force, from which all physical and mental powers are derived. In some images, in place of mace, the bow, arrows and quiver are shown. The bow called Sarnga represents ego, the origin of sensorial perception, which means that it is the symbol of the divine power of illusion (Maya), while the numerous arrows of Vishnu are the senses, the fields of activity of the intellect and the quiver is the store-house of actions.

The worshippers of Vishnu, known as Vaishnavas, recognise in him the Supreme Being, out of whom emerge Brahma, the active creator, Vishnu himself the preserver; and Shiva or Rudra, the destructor. Vishnu's preserving, restoring and protecting powers have been manifest on earth in a variety of forms, called Avataras, in which one or more portions of his divine attributes were embodied in the shapes of a human being or an animal or a human-animal combined form, possessing great and sometimes supernatural powers. All these Avataras of Vishnu appeared in the world either to correct some great evil or to effect some great good on the earth. These incarnations are ten in number, though Bhagvata Purana increases them to twenty two and adds further that they are innumerable.

However out of the ten universally recognised incarnations, nine are said to have appeared on the earth while the tenth is yet to descend here.

The first of these is Matsya (fish) incarnation. According to Hindu mythology the universe is subject to a cycle of periodical destruction and thereafter new creation. Before the latest creation, that is of the present universe, the four Vedas (the holy books from the mouth of the Supreme-Deity) were immersed in the waters. It was necessary to get hold of them to instruct Brahma about the work of creation. Vishnu was therefore appointed to bring up the Vedas from the deep. He took the form of a fish (Matsya), descended into the water and brought-up these sacred books.

The second is Kachyup or Kurma (tortoise) incarnation. In this Vishnu assumed the form of a tortoise and took the newly created earth upon his back in order to render this trembling globe a stability. The belief is held that to this hour the earth is supported on the back of this tortoise.

The third incarnation is that of Varaha (boar). In periodical destructions of the world, once the earth sunk into the deep waters, Vishnu, the great preserver, taking the form of a boar descended into the waters and drew up the earth with the help of his tusks.

The fourth incarnation is that of Narasimha (half-lion half-man combine). This peculiar form was adopted by Vishnu to kill a demoniac ruler, named Hiranyakashipu, who pleased god Brahma, by his religious sacrifices who in turn blessed him with a boon that no known man or animal, born in the natural process could kill him, that he could not die either in the day or in the night, on the earth or in heavens, either by fire, by water or by any weapon. It was to kill such a tyrant and to remove him from the earth that Vishnu assumed the form of Narasimha, which was neither man nor animal; came out of a broken pillar, laid hold of the demon-king by its teeth, put him up on his thighs and tore him up in the middle by his claws; it was evening time-neither day nor night. This incarnation demands separate treatment in some detail because Narasimha is still worshipped as a full fledged deity in many parts of India.

The fifth incarnation is that of Vamana (the dwarf). The fourth lineal descendant of Hiranyakashipu, named Bali, through his devotion and penance defeated Indra, the god of the firmament, humbled other gods and extended his authority over the three worlds. All the gods appealed to Vishnu for protection and he became manifest in the dwarf Avatara of Vamana for the purpose of restraining Bali. Once when this King was making a great religious sacrifice, Vishnu in the form of Vamana appeared before him for gifts in the company of other Brahmanas. Bali was extremely pleased to see a holy man in such a diminutive form and promised to give him whatever he asked. Vishnu asked only for as much land as he could measure by three steps. Bali laughingly agreed to grant the boon of three steps. Vishnu as a dwarf stepped over heaven in the first stride and then on earth in the second stride. Then out of respect to Bali's kindness and his grandfather Prahlada's great virtues, Vishnu stopped short and left to him Patal, the subterranian region.

The sixth incarnation is that of Parsuram. Parsu is the name of an axe-like weapon owned by this incarnation. This incarnation came as a Brahman, who manifested himself at the close of the Satyayuga (the first great millenium of Hindu mythological time calculus). This appearance was for the purpose of repressing the tyranny of the power-drunk Kshatriya-caste. This sixth Avatara of Vishnu appeared in the world before Rama, the seventh Avatara, but they are both represented to be living at the same time.

When the Kshatriya kings of the earth and their ministers became very corrupt and committed all sorts of sins, the goddess Prithvi (Mother-Earth) went to Vishnu and prayed for relief. Her petition was accepted and Vishnu appeared on the earth as a descendant of great sage Bhrigoo. To avenge the gruesome murder of his father by a Kshatriya King and the great oppression perpetrated by rulers he is said to have cleared the earth of the Kshtriyas twenty one times and filled with their blood five large lakes. He is said to be instrumental in colonising much of Southern India, where so many shrines are dedicated to him.

The seventh and eighth Avatars of Vishnu are those of most famous heroes of mythology, Ram and Krishna. Ram was the son of Dashrath, king of Ayodhya, who appeared to destroy the arch-demon Ravan, while Krishna, deemed to be the most perfect avatar of Vishnu, came to the world to kill evil doers and to establish the rule of righteousness. These two incarnations are the best known and most popular gods amongst the Hindus everywhere and have been dealt with elsewhere independently.

The ninth Avatar is that of Balram, also known as Bala-Bhadra of Bala-Deva, the elder brother of Krishna. The story in Mahabharat narrates that Vishnu too two hairs, a white and a black one, that these became Balram and Krishna, the two children of Devaki. He was so powerful that he, single-handedly, at a very tender age killed the great demon, Asur Dhenuka, who had the form of an ass. Another demon tried to carry off Balram on his shoulders but the young boy beat out the demon's brain with his fists. When Krishna went to Mathura, Balram accompanied him and manfully supported him till Kans was killed by his younger brothers. He also taught both Duryodhan and Bhim the use of the mace. His chief weapon is Ploughshare (hal) and he is therefore named Haldhar too.

Those who hold the view that Balram is not the incarnation of Vishnu but of the great serpent Sesha on whom Vishnu reclines, claim that the ninth Avatar of Vishnu is Buddha. In this case the phenomenal success of Buddha as a religious teacher seems to have persuaded the

Brahmans to adopt him as one member of their own pantheon of gods.

The tenth and the last incarnation of Vishnu that is yet to appear in the world at the end of the Kaliyuga or the Machine Age is that of Kalki. This Avatara shall appear seated on a white horse with a drawn sword blazing like a comet. He shall come to finally destroy the wicked, to restart the new creation and to restore the purity of conduct in people's lives.

All the above incarnations are only the earthly manifestation of Vishnu, who himself is eternal, unchangeable and immutable. He is blue-skinned and in all pictures, images and reliefs he is seen in rich ornaments and regal garments. His wife is Lakshmi or Sri, the goddess of wealth and fortune. His place of abode is Vaikuntha (heaven) and his vehicle is Garuda, a giant-sized eagle which often is shown as a winged, human-shaped figure having a beak-like nose. Vishnu is the infinite ocean from which the world emerges. Hence his symbol is water (Nara) and he himself is called 'Narayana' - the one who dwells upon the waters.[1] He is depicted as reclining under a many-headed snake, as mentioned above, and this denotes Ananta Nag (the timeless or ageless snake). From his navel grows the lotus out of which appears Brahma, the god who created the universe.

Such is Supreme God Vishnu, the all-pervading divinity, who descends as an Avatara (incarnation) to establish the rule of law and order of justice in each important age of the world's history.

---

[1]Lord Vishnu, the preserver of noble life is also known by the epithet 'Narayana' which is symbolic and implies that as water is essential for the survival of life, so is he.

Lord Shivji

Lord Shiva — represents the complete cyclic process of generation, destruction and regeneration. The all embracing nature of Lord Shiva is reflected in his 1008 names.

SHIVA

Shiva meaning 'the Good God is the third member of the triad. He is also named as Mahesh or Mahadeva (the Greatest God). He is many-sided and multi-colourful as compared to many of the other gods including Vishnu.

Shiva is represented in various ways, but the distinctive characteristics of this god are (1) his seat, which is invariably either the skin of a tiger or a panther, (2) a number of cobras all around his neck and shoulders, (3) his long matted hair tied into a mop atop his head, (4) the crescent that he wears on the mop of his hair, (5) the sacred river Ganga falling upon his head and flowing by his side, (6) the trident (trishula), the symbol of his power, (7) the sacred bull, and (8) the mendicant's bowl.[1]

Besides these symbols another very important physical characteristic of Shiva is his vertical third eye. In the Mahabharata, the great Hindu epic, the legend of how Shiva got the third eye is given this way. One day his beautiful consort Parvati (daughter of the King of

---

[1]'These belongings made many scholars believe that originally Lord Shiva was considered as the God of the primitives and it was much later, that the Aryans accepted him in the fold of the Sanatan or the Hindu pantheon.

Mountains), stealthily went behind Shiva and playfully placed her hands over his eyes. Suddenly darkness engulfed the whole world and all beings trembled in great fear as the lord of the universe had closed his eyes. Suddenly a massive tongue of flame leapt from the forehead of Shiva; a third eye appeared there and this gave light to the world.

In Sri Shiva Tattva this eye is described as the frontal eye or the eye of fire, and it is the eye of higher perception. It looks mainly inward but whenever directed outward, it burns all that appears before it. It is from a glance of the third eye that Kama, the lord of lust, was burnt to ashes and that the gods and all created beings were destroyed at each of the periodical destruction of the universe. Hence Shiva is also called Tri-netra, Tri-ambaka, Tri-aksha or Tri-nayana because of his three eyes. About the different symbols surrounding Lord Shiva, the scriptures give various explanations.

(a) The tiger skin: The tiger is the vehicle of Shakti, the goddess of all power and force. Shiva is beyond and above any kind of force. He is its master and carries the skin of the tiger as the victor of every force. According to an interesting legend in Purana, once Shiva wandered in the forests in the form of a bare-bodied mendicant and the wives of the sages were enchanted by his figure. The jealous and angry sages tried to capture him by digging a pit and when Shiva passed by that pit, a tiger was made to rush out of it. Shiva slew that tiger, took its skin and wore it as a garment.

(b) Cobras around the neck: Shiva is beyond the power of death though he is surrounded and encircled by death. This aspect is also emphasised by his name Nilakantha, the god who alone can drink the deadly poison to free the world from its effects. The cobras around his neck also represent the basic dormant energy, which is called Kundalini, the serpent power.

(c) Matted hair: The flowing Jata or matted hair of Shiva represents him as the lord of wind, Vayu, who is the subtle form of breath all round.

(d) Crescent on hair-mop : He bears on his head as a diadem the crescent of the fifth day moon. This is placed near the fiery third eye and this shows the power of Soma, the sacrificial offering, which is the representative of Moon. It means that Shiva possesses the power of procreation co-existent with that of destruction.

(e) Sacred Ganga: The holiest of the holy rivers, namely Ganga, flowing from the crown of Shiva's head represents the causal waters, from which the earth arises. It also represents the essential instrument of ritual purification. By holding the Ganges on his head, Shiva allowed an outlet to the great holy river to traverse the earth and bring purifying water to the human beings.

(f) The Trident: The Trishula of Shiva is the symbol of the three functions of the Creator, the Preserver and the Destroyer. This also represents the instrument of punishment to the evil doer on all the three planes, viz., spiritual, subtle and physical.

In popular representations Shiva stands majestically in the centre of the universe, adorned with all his symbols-the crescent, cobras, prayer beads, the trident and matted hair. Very often a female figure-head adorns his head; she is goddess Ganga who was brought from heavens by Bhagiratha and as earth could not bear Ganga's impact, she was taken by Shiva on his own head. At other times Shiva is shown as riding on his bull, called Nandi, covered with ashes all over his body, his eyes inflamed with intoxicating herbs and with a drum and a horn in his two hands. The ashes on the body symbolise him as a Yogi, who has burnt all his evil desires and rubbed himself with the ashes of the ritual fire. Shiva's bull, Nandi (the joyful) is white as snow with a huge body and soft brown eyes. Its hump resembles the top of a snow-covered mountain. The bull represents lust or the sexual impulse and Shiva is the master of lust fully controlling it by riding on its back.

Another well-known name of Shiva is Rudra. In the Vedas, Rudra is called by many names and has many attributes. He is considered as the roaring god, the terrible god, and the god of storm and tempest. On the one hand, if angry, he can bring disaster to man and his wealth of cattle but if pleased he can be kind and beneficent. In Yajur Veda, Rudra is also called 'Mahadeva', a name specifically applied today only to Shiva. According to Vishnu Purana this god Rudra is said to have sprung from the forehead of Brahma and later separated himself into male and female. This legend is the forerunner of Shiva's another manifestation, called Ardhanarishvara, where he is half-male and half-female, combining energies of both the sexes.

The image of Ardhanarishwara, represents Lord Shiva as the union of substance and energy, the life principle and Shakti. Vishnu Purana says that Rudra is also given seven other names by Brahma- Bhava, Sarva, Ishana, Pashupati, Bhima, Ugra and Mahadeva. Shiva is also known by all these names. Hence, gradually Rudra of Vedas ceased to have any separate identity and became completely merged into Shiva.

Shiva represents the complete cyclic process of generation, destruction and regeneration. The all-embracing nature of this god is reflected in 1008 names given to him in scriptures and in the mind of numerous Hindus he is in essence not different from the Vedic notion of the multiple forms of a single divine power.

Shiva is also known by the popular name-Nataraja, the lord of the cosmic dance. Numerous images of Shiva in his dancing pose are available throughout India and this image of Shiva is also the most popular of Indian gods amongst the foreigners. The small drum of Lord Shiva is the symbol of rhythm and sound. In fact rhythm is there in the whole movement of the universe and sound is the medium, musical and divine, that comes from the word of the Supreme Deity, and carries revelations and the truth. Sound with atmospheric ether also represents the primeval outburst of creation.

Shiva is known by numerous names as mentioned earlier, like, Shankar[1] the Giver of Joy; Shambhu, the Abode of Joy. As Maheshwar, he is the Divine Lord, the source of knowledge. In him are co-ordinated the three energies from which knowledge flows, the power of understanding (Jnana), the will (Iccha) and the action (Kriya). Shiva is Mahakala, which means not only the Lord of Death but more correctly

---

[1]Shankar literally means one who subdues all equally.

the Lord of Time. Before anything could come to exist, time has to be present. In fact time is the first condition for the existence of the world for it is prior to space.

Shiva's another well known name is Yogiraja, i.e., the Lord of Yoga. He is himself represented as the perfect or the greatest ascetic. His is the last word in austerity, penance and meditation. His method of Yoga is different from rituals and therefore in some earlier Hindu scriptures, Shiva is accused of teaching the secrets of higher truths to those who are low-born or who are not properly qualified for ritual practices. To Lord Shiva is attributed, the revelation to mankind the method and technique of Yoga, which in these days are very popular in the West.

In many images of Shiva five faces are depicted, each looking towards each direction that is East, West, North, South and finally one looking upward. The five faces represent five aspects. The face looking upward is called Ishana (the Ruler), and is copper-coloured. He is the embodiment of all forms of learnings and represents the enjoyer of nature (Kshetrajan). The eastern face of Shiva is called Tat-purusha (the Supreme Man) and is yellow-coloured. It represents all nature connected with earth, the sense of smell and the anus as the organ of action. The western face of Shiva is red and is called Vamadeva (the Left-hand Deity), it represents ego (Ahamkara) and corresponds to the element-fire. It is connected with the sense of sight. The southern face of Shiva is blue or sometimes blue-black, it is called Aghora Bhairava (the Frightful), it represents intellect (Buddhi) and eternal laws (Dharma). It is connected with the sense of hearing and the organ of speech. The northern face of Shiva is called Sdyọjat (the suddenly born) and is white in colour. It represents the mind and corresponds to sacrificial elixir (Soma).

Amongst the above five faces the southern face of Shiva, called Aghora-Bhairava needs a brief explanation. As indicated above, Bhairava means 'Frightful', Terrible'. Lord Shiva, after the death of his first wife 'Sati' could not be consoled. He wandered over the earth aimlessly carrying the corpse of his consort on his shoulders. To bring back Shiva to his normal state and to relieve him from obsession, Vishnu with his Sudarshana Chakra cut up Sati's body scattering her limbs at various spots. The places where the limbs fell became sacred spots and are known as Shaktipithas. Each of these spots is guarded by Shiva in the form of a Bhairava. Bhairava is seen either in the company of a dog or riding a dog. Bhairava is invoked in rites designed to destroy enemies.

Another most popular image of Shiva has no human form but is represented by Linga (Phallus figure). It is made of black or white stone, depicted sometimes as 'rounded both at top and bottom to show that it does not stand' or 'arise from' anywhere in our space or time, and in some cases, as an egg-shaped stone, tapering at top recalling either the 'Cosmic Egg', from which the world emerged or the 'Bright Flame of Light'; hence it is called Jyotir Linga too. Thus whether depicted as the generative symbol or the fountain-source of light, this Linga represents the Lord of the Universe.

It may also be noted that sex symbolism is for long associated with farming and the implements connected with it. This fertility aspect of the Linga belongs to the period of epics and puranas. As the symbol of transcendental energy and power, Linga is the central conception of Shiva's philosophy. Shiva is represented in temples in beautifully sculptured forms as well the symbolic Linga form. Amongst the lingayat sect followers, the initiation ceremony corresponding to the sacred thread ceremony of most of the Hindus is performed by replacing Yajnopavita (the sacred thread) with a necklace of small Lingas. In south India, a formalised miniature Linga, attached to necklace and concealed under the clothing, is also worn by male devotees of Shiva.

In fact, the phallus aspect has been overdone by western scholars though Linga actually means a 'sign', 'mark' or 'symbol'. Shiva-Purana, the source book of Shiva's divinity, itself defines Linga as "the distinctive sign through which it is possible to recognise the nature of the object." Thus Linga, the phallus or the giver of life is the important shape under which the nature of the shapeless can be represented. Again Shiva-Purana in another hymn says: "It is not the Linga itself which is worshipped but the owner of the Linga, the Progenitor, the Supreme Creator (Purushottam). The Linga leads to Shiva, who is symbolised by it". The Shiva-Linga is represented erect and is divided into three parts. The lowest part is below the pedestal, and is called brahma part. The middle or the second part is on the pedestal and is womb-shaped: it is called Vishnu part. The third part is cylindrical and above the pedestal which is the Rudra-Shiva part.

Shivaratri, i.e., Shiva's Night is the famous festival in honour of Lord Shiva. It is held on the fourteenth night of the dark half moon in the month of Magha (January-February). Throughout the night Shiva's image is showered with green leaves. This custom is based on a legend, which states that, once a hunter after his game in a thick forest lost the way and decided to spend the night on a tree. He could not sleep properly due to cold, and feeling uneasy he kept on changing postures. With his movements the leaves kept on falling below, where a Shiva-Linga stood at the foot of the tree. The Lord was so pleased with him that he bestowed upon him good fortunes. Hence the custom of holding this night-festival, of Shivaratri.

Shiva is deified due to the assimilation of many facets of human activity in him. He is considered to be the god of destruction and the personification of the disintegrative forces of the cosmos. Many bloody rites are associated with his worship. He is the god of regeneration and sexuality. Some of Hinduism's potent symbols are associated with Shiva.

Shiva is also considered to be the god of asceticism and is called Mahayogi or 'great yogi'. Certain legends hold the view that he was condemned to perpetual asceticism for cutting off the fifth head of Brahma when he was disrespectful to him.

Shiva is also considered to be the god of the terrible, a flesh-eater, demanding sacrifices (of human beings, animals etc.), the lord of the cruel and evil side of things, haunting cemetries, attended by host of pramatha, sprites, goblins, spirits, ghosts, vetala or vampires which haunt cemetries, animate dead bodies and feed on human blood.

Kirtimukha was the terrible demon and the most hideous member of his entourage. He was created by Shiva to fight Rahu who once opposed him. When Rahu saw Kirtimukha he begged for mercy and at Shiva's command the monster desisted. But in order to fulfil the demand of the demon for a meal, Shiva offered his own feet. The monster ate his feet, his legs, belly, chest and arms till only the head remained. Shaivites use the grotesque face of Kirtimukha as a talisman.

Shiva is known by 1008 names or epithets. Most popular of them are: Adinatha (first lord); Asitanga (black limbed); Babhru (brown); Baleshvera (hair-lord); Bhairom (modern variant of Bhairava); Bhava (existence) Bhuteshvara (demon-lord); Chandra-chuda or Chandra-shekara (moon-crested); Dhurjati (mat haired); Ekambareshvara (one-garmented or nude); Gajasamhara (elephant-destroyer); Gangadhara (Ganges bearer); Ghrisheshvara (rubbing lord); Girisha (mountain-lord); Hara (seizer); Hatakeshvara (ruler of the Hataka people); Hiranya-retas (having golden semen); Jambukeshvara (lord of Jambu or India); Jata-dhara (mat-haired); Kala (black or time); Kalasamhara (time slayer); Kapalamalin (skull garlanded); Kapaleshvara (skull lord); Kedar nath (mountain lord); Kritti-vasas (skin clad); Krodha (wrathful); Mahadeva (great lord); Mahakala (dissolver of time); Maheshvara (great lord); Mrityunjaya (death-destroyer); Nataraja or Nadesa (dance-lord); Panchanana (five faced); Prapitamaheshvara (great grandfather god); Sadashiva (eternal Shiva); Sthanu (immoveable); Shulabhrit (endowed with Shula); Shulapani (holding Shula); Svashva (whose horse is a dog); Tamrachuda (red-crested); Tribhuvaneshvara (three-world lord); Tripurantaka (triple world ender); Ugra-deva (fierce god); Vajreshvara (thunderbolt lord); Vishvanatha or Visveshvara (universal lord); Vaidyanatha (physician lord); Virupaksha (having ill-formed eyes); Visalaksha (large eyed); Yogeshvara (lord of Yoga).

RAMACHANDRA

Lord Rama is the seventh Avatara (incarnation) of Vishnu. Born during the second age of the world called Treta Yuga, he is the immortal hero of the great religious epic of India, the Ramayana. This epic seems to have been written sometime between the fifth and the first century B.C.though stories of Rama's noble life were known to the residents of this land much earlier.

Rama occupies a very reverential place in the religious life of India and in the religious history of the world. He is the embodiment of righteousness and is believed to be the incarnation of the solar aspect of Vishnu. The most ancient and the most striking of the tales of Ramachandra is the Ramayana, written by sage Valmiki, who is also considered as the father of epic style of poetry.

Innumerable temples are scattered all over India with the images of Rama, his younger brother Lakshmana and his consort, Sita. In all images Rama is invariably depicted to be having two arms and not four, which emphasises the character of Rama as a human being and the way god Vishnu preferred to adopt this form just to re-establish the golden age of justice and happiness. The expression of Rama Rajya even today means the reign in which peace and prosperity prevails.

Rama lived during the end of the Treta Yuga or the second age of the world, when the sages, the holy men and even gods were terrorized and alarmed by the misdeeds of Ravana, the demoniac king of Lanka, and the horde of his followers. Ravana had pleased Brahma by austere penance and Brahma had given him the boon of invulnerability from the wrath of any god or goddess. Thus being fortified Ravana started his reign of terror and misused his power to terrorise people in order to subdue them. All the gods then decided to approach Brahma to seek help to relieve themselves from the looming danger and deliver the sages from their sufferings. Brahma disclosed to them that Ravana, in his pride, thought that since gods could not overpower him, no one else could subdue him and that Ravana was actually destined to due at the hands of a god in human form.

The gods now reached Vishnu to whom they prayed for deliverance because he was responsible for the preservation of heavenly and earthly order. Vishnu promised to descend on the earth in the form of a man by taking birth as a son to Dasharatha, a king of the solar race, reigning at Ayodhya. So once when King Dasharatha was performing a religious sacrifice, the fire-god emerged before him out of the sacred fire and gave him a pot of nectar for his three wives to drink. King Dasharatha gave half of this nectar to his seniormost wife, Kaushalya, who brought forth Rama endowed with one half of the divine essence; a quarter to Kaikeyi, the second wife, whose son Bharata was endowed with a quarter of divine essence; and the fourth part to Sumitra, the juniormost wife, who brought forth two sons, Lakshmana and Shatrughna, each having one eighth part of divinity. All four brothers were deeply attached to each other but Lakshmana was more devoted to Rama and Shatrughna to Bharata. Lord Vishnu thus kept his word to the gods and was born as Prince Rama in the household of King Dasharatha.

Another legend gives the version that Dasharatha divided the divine nectar between his two senior wives, Kaushalya and Kaikeyi only and that when the younger, Sumitra, asked for some, each of the senior ones gave one half from their respective shares. So Sumitra received two quarters and gave birth to two sons-one part received from Kaushalya resulted in the birth of Lakshmana who was always attached to Rama and the other part received from Kaikeyi resulted in the birth of Shatrughna who was more attracted towards Bharata.

All the four brothers grew up together at Ayodhya and learnt various subjects covering arts of peace and methods of wars at a very fast pace. While they were still young and Rama had turned only sixteen, one highly revered saint, named Vishvamitra, came to king Dasharatha. He requested for Rama's help to protect him and his disciples from demons, who were interfering with his usual religious sacrifices to gods. Very reluctantly Dasharatha sent Rama and his younger son Lakshmana to the hermitage of sage Vishvamitra. Rama cleared the hermitage of all demons and killed a powerful female-demon named Taraka. Sage Vishvamitra was very pleased and taught Rama precious pieces of rare wisdom. He also gave Rama some celestial weapons with extraordinary powers.

On their way back to the kingdom of Ayodhya. Vishvamitra took the two brothers to the court of king Janaka, the ruler of Mithila (a territory near Ayodhya). King Janaka at this time was making preparations for the marriage of his beautiful daughter Sita. He wanted to marry her off to a talented and strong prince and so he had arranged a competition as a prelude to Sita's marriage. Janaka had in his possession a divine bow which he received as gift from Lord Shiva and he announced before the assembly of the competing princes that anyone who could lift the bow and stretch its string, would win the hand of his daughter. But none except Rama could succeed, who stretched this bow with such force that it broke into two pieces. Thus Sita was married to Rama amidst joy and gaiety.

The breaking of Shiva's divine bow by Rama was followed by an interesting episode. Parsuram, the sixth incarnation of Vishnu, who was alive at that time (to take revenge against Kshatriyas for the murder of his father), reached the court of King Janaka just at that moment. When he saw the broken bow he became furious and started rebuking the prince of Ayodhya. He challenged Rama for a combat and settle the score. However the dispute was ultimately settled peacefully and Parsuram too was convinced of the greatness of Rama.

Rama reached back to Ayodhya along with Sita and Lakshmana. king Dasharatha now felt that he had been growing old. So, he decided to formally announce the name of his eldest son Rama as the next successor to his throne. But at this time an unjust and undesirable thing occurred. Kaikeyi, the second and the most favourite wife of Dasharatha, had a hunch-backed maid-servant, named Manthara. She was crooked not only in body but in mind too. Though Kaikeyi, like a good step-mother, loved Rama without malice, this female slave Manthara, played the role of a wicked court lady and, worked upon the maternal instincts of Kaikeyi. Manthara poisoned the mind of Kaikeyi against her step son Rama and instigated her to secure a promise from the king that her son Bharata would be made the heir apparent to the kingdom. All this aroused her base instincts and Kaikeyi decided to defeat Dasharatha's plan of declaring Rama as the next king of Ayodhya. She remembered the past when king Dasharatha, infatuated by her charms and feeling grateful on account of her courage in saving his life, had promised to grant her two boons. So now, she remonstrated with her husband and reminded him of his word of honour given earlier. She asked him to declare Bharata as the next king of Ayodhya and also to send away Rama for fourteen years in exile away from Ayodhya. After a prolonged argument, finally with utmost reluctance the king yielded to the pressure and agreed to send Rama into exile for fourteen years and to install Bharata on the throne of Ayodhya in his place.

Rama, as an obedient son, accepted his father's order went away leaving behind his parents and the people of Ayodhya. He together with his wife Sita moved towards the south. His younger brother, Lakshmana, the son of Sumitra, also accompanied both of them. All the three settled at Chitrakut in the Dandak forest between the Yamuna and the Godavari rivers. King Dasharatha could not bear this shock and departed from the world. At this time Bharata and Shatrughna had gone for a visit to the fomer's maternal uncle. Both of them were called back and Bharata was asked to ascend the throne. Bharata vehemently opposed the idea of becoming the king stating that the rightful heir to the throne was the eldest brother, Ramachandra. Bharata together with numerous courtiers and enthusiastic people of Ayodhya set out towards the forest to bring Rama, Sita and Lakshmana back to Ayodhya. When both the brothers met, there ensued a long argument. Rama declined to return to the kingdom without completing the exile term of fourteen years while Bharata did not agree to sit on the throne. It was finally agreed that Bharata should return and act as Rama's vicegerent for the time being till the completion of exile. Bharata carried Rama's footwears to Ayodhya as a sign of regard and obeisance to the elder brother and he placed it at the foot of the throne as a mark of recognition to Rama's supremacy.

For a period of ten years Rama together with his wife and brother moved in the forests from one hermitage to another. Then he met sage Agastya near the Vindhyachal mountains, who advised Rama to set up his abode at Panchavati near the banks of river Godavari. So, Rama with Sita and Lakshmana got settled at Panchavati which was adjacent to the regions inhabited by Rakshasas (demoniac tribes) and had been attracting periodical visits by them. Once Surpanakha, sister of the mighty demon king of Lanka, named Ravana, visited the place and was enchanted by the physical beauty of Rama. When she made advances, Rama rebuked her. When she made scurrilous remarks against Sita, Lakshmana could not control his rage and chopped off the nose of Surpanakha. To avenge this insult she returned accompanied by her two brothers, Khara and Dushana, who also brought a big army along with them. In the battle both the brothers of Surpanakha were defeated and their army routed.

When her mission was thwarted Surpanakha retired to Lanka, where her mightiest brother was the ruler. She wept before Ravana and pleaded to avenge those who heaped humiliation upon her. Ravana took his best confidant Maricha with him and made plans to teach Rama a lesson. Maricha lured Rama away from the hermitage on a hunting expedition by posing himself as the prey. Lakshmana was left alone to guard Sita. But Maricha somehow lured Lakshmana too on a mission to search Rama. Thus when Sita was left alone Ravana disguised as a Sadhu (Mendicant) forcibly kidnapped Sita from her hut in Panchavati.

The anger and sorrow of Rama at the disappearance of Sita knew no bounds. He determined to trace his wife and punish the culprits. He and Lakshmana started the search in right earnest. On the way they won the friendship of the chieftain of monkey tribe. His name was Sugriva, whose capital, Kishkindhya, was usurped by his own brother Bali. Rama killed Bali and restored the throne to Sugriva. This paved the way for solid alliance that helped Rama in a great way in his battle against Ravana and his forces. As a result of this friendship Rama not only got massive support of the huge army of Sugriva but also found a highly loyal and efficient general named Hanuman, who proved to be the greatest asset to Rama.

To prove his gratitude to Rama, Sugriva sent a great number of his monkeys in search of Sita. These monkeys went towards South and found out that the demon Ravana had stolen Sita and kept her as his captive in Lanka. Immediately Hanuman became ready to go to her as Rama's emissary. Rama gave his ring to Hanuman to convince Sita of the latter's genuine status. As Hanuman was the offspring of the god of winds, he concentrated his powers and leaped across so many miles over the sea. He found Sita kept as a prisoner in a garden of roses, called Ashok-vatika. He showed her the ring of Rama and assured her that he would be soon coming to rescue Sita from the clutches of Ravana.

Meanwhile Ravana's guards managed to catch Hanuman and brought him to the court of Ravana. As the legend goes, before being caught Hanuman succeeded in killing so many guards including one of the sons of Ravana, named Akshaya. Then Ravana's mightiest son, Indrajit was send who succeeded in bringing the monkey general before Ravana. The king ordered his servants to dip the monkey's tail in oil and set it on fire. The enraged Hanuman with his enflamed tail leaped from one house to the other thus setting so many of them aflame. Eventually he left Lanka and reached Rama's camp to give him the news regarding the plight of Sita.

Now Rama and Lakshmana together with the big army of monkeys proceeded to invade Lanka. When they reached the seashore, Rama first worshipped Lord Shiva and prayed for the success of his mission. He then requested the ocean to devise some way so that he with his vast army could cross the sea and invade Lanka. The ocean appeared before Rama and replied, "Lord Rama, every element has certain nature of its own and it cannot be altered. I cannot dry the water-bed to help you. The only way to cross me is by building a bridge. Among the army personnel of yours there is one ape named Nala. He is the son of the god of construction, Vishvakarman and Nala has a blessing that whatever he would throw in the water would not sink but float." At the command of Nala, rocks were brought and he threw them into the sea. A long bridge was thus built connecting Lanka with the shore on Rama's side. Rama together with his army crossed the sea and reached the outskirts of Lanka.

When Rama and his soldiers reached Lanka there ensued a fierce fighting. Many of the mighty generals of Ravana and a great number of his soldiers were killed in the battles. Then came forward Kumbhakarna, the younger brother of Ravana who was like a giant and valourous as a lion, and he fought bravely against Rama and his allies. He started devouring the monkeys but when the giant put them in his mouth, the agile monkeys came out from his ears and nostrils. Rama first cut off his arms, then his legs his bow and arrow. Still he waddled round and continued the fight. Eventually Rama gave him a fatal wound in the neck.

Then came Indrajit, the son of Ravana. In this battle Rama's brother, Lakshmana, was severely wounded and became unconscious. The physician prescribed an herb that could save the life of Lakshmana. But it grew far away on one of the mountains in the Himalayas and someone had to fetch it before the daybreak. The agile Hanuman undertook the task and he flew towards the Himalayas with the speed of wind. He brought the herb, and the life of Lakshmana was saved in time. In the dramatic fight later, Indrajit was also defeated and killed.

Now Ravana himself entered the field of battle. After fierce fighting that lasted many days, Ravana was slain and victory ensued. Sita was thus rescued from the clutches of Ravana. Rama desired that Sita should pass through a fiery ordeal to prove her innocence. Rama did this to convince all skeptics about his wife's purity rather than to assure himself. After her innocence was proved, Rama, Sita and Lakshmana returned to Ayodhya. This story of Rama has also got an interesting epilogue.

Rama ascended the throne and started ruling over Ayodhya. However some persons in the capital commenced a slander campaign alleging that it was not proper for Rama to shelter Sita after she had been kept by a demon king in his captivity. Rama, therefore, sent Sita in exile. She found refuge in the hermitage of sage Valmiki, where she gave birth to two sons, Lava and Kusha. Before long Rama performed the horse sacrifice ceremony, enjoined upon brave kings by holy scriptures. During this ceremony the two sons of Rama, Lava and Kusha, challenged their father's supremacy and their identity was eventually disclosed. Rama wanted to repeat the old fire-ordeal in front of the people of his kingdom to prove the fidelity of his wife. However Prithvi (the earth), the mother of Sita, opened her bosom and took back her daughter to the great remorse and lamentation of Rama. After completing his mission Rama too left his material body and went back to his heavenly abode.

The festivals associated with Rama's incarnation and celebrated in India are Rama Navimi, Diwali and Dussehra. The first one is associated with the birth of Lord Rama, the seventh incarnation of Vishnu. The birthday of Rama which falls on the ninth day of the Hindu month Chaitra, is celebrated in almost all Vaishnava temples. Congregations are organised, sermons delivered and songs are sung by devotees.

Dussehra is the culmination of the ten-day celebrations, organised to exhibit the episodes from the life of Lord Rama. For the first nine days the whole story of Rama is enacted onstage with great pomp and show. On the tenth day the last episode of Rama's victory over Ravana is shown and the effigies of Ravana, his brother Kumbhakarna and his son Indrajit are burnt amidst loud rejoicing. In all the big cities of U.P., Bihar M.P., Delhi and Mysore this festival is a day of mass celebrations. Lakhs of people gather in vast fields and open spaces to witness the burning of the effigies and the fire works following the same.

Diwali is celebrated, in commemoration of the day on which Rama was crowned after his return to Ayodhya with Sita. As Rama had ascended the throne on this day, king Vikrama, who probably started the custom of lighting lamps as a part of Diwali festival, selected the same auspicious day for his coronation too. Diwali is the most important festival of the trading community in Western India, where money is spent lavishly on this day. Sweets are distributed amongst friends and relatives; public buildings in cities are beautifully illuminated and children are supplied with a good stock of crackers which they burst till late hours in the night. Houses are cleansed and neatly whitewashed while in business houses new account books are started.

According to one of the Upanishads, named Rama-purv-tapni Upanishad, "Just as the whole nature of the large banyan tree is contained in its tiny seed, so also the whole universe moving and unmoving, is contained in the seed-word Rama".

Certain legends hold the view that Rama refused to have Sita back as his queen since she had been associated with another man. It is said that even after proving her innocence by mounting the pyre and emerging unhurt, he was not satisfied. It was Rama who banished his wife, unable to bear any further insinuation. She was heavy with child at the time of banishment and gave birth to twin sons Lava and Kusha at the hermitage of the sage Valmiki.

It was only after a lapse of fifteen years that Rama and Sita encountered each other. Once Rama was performing an ashvamedha yajna, when he came across his brave sons. He became reconciled to Sita and persuaded her to return to Ayodhaya. But she asked her mother Earth to receive her back, whereupon the earth opened up and swallowed her.

Rama was filled with remorse and he was unable to endure life without his wife. The grieving Rama resolved to end his life but was saved by Lakshmana. When Lakshmana also left the earthly abode, Rama felt disconsolate and lonely and walked into the river Sarayu. There he entered into the glory of Vishnu. There, it is believed that

Sita, in the form of Lakshmi sits by his side, both remaining united forever.

The worship of Rama is universal in India. Inspite of a few blemishes and his attitude towards his wife, he is considered to be a perfect hero since he was the husband of a single wife, devoted, affectionate and brave. He was also a perfect ruler, for his reign at Ayodhya was considered to be a golden age of perfect peace and prosperity, and is proverbial for a happy and just rule. Due to all these reasons it is believed that his worship never degenerates into impurity and licentiousness.

Lord Krishnji

KRISHNA

Krishna, the god who delivered the message of Gita to Arjuna, is worshipped in thousands of temples throughout India. As a lovable child, as a shrewd diplomat, as a great sage and even as fearless man of action, Krishna's personality has fascinated for ages not only Indians but also thinkers of other lands.

Krishna's picture is depicted in so many styles; in fact Lord Krishna has probably been the subject of numerous masterpieces of art. Sometimes he is shown as a child eating butter-cake, at other times he is seen dancing with maidens or playing on flute or advising Arjuna in the battlefield of Kurukshetra, so on and so forth.

The story of Krishna starts with the marriage of his parents. He was born in the Yadava clan, who was a group of brave and virile people. There was a branch of this clan called Shoora and Vasudeva, Krishna's father was their chief. At the same time there was another tribe living adjacently and their chief was King Ugrasen. The first son of this king was Kansa, a villainous character. Elders of the two tribes were anxious to forge an alliance. King Ugrasen's brother named Devak had a beautiful daughter named Devaki, who was married with Vasudeva to ensure peace between the two tribes.

Kansa was cruel, haughty and wicked. Once sags Narada, predicted that the eighth child of Devaki would slay Kansa. When Kansa heard this, he decided to kill not only the eighth child but all the children of Devaki immediately after birth. To implement his diabolical plan, Kansa held both Vasudeva and Devaki as prisoners in the palace. This way six of Devaki's sons were killed by Kansa one by one. The seventh son of Devaki was saved by her husband's kinsmen, who took away the child, immediately after birth to a nearby town named Gokul at the house of his friend, Nand, where Vasudeva's elder wife, Rohini, was living.

As the fateful day of the birth of the eighth child drew near, Devaki was full of anxiety. She had been told by a great sage that Lord Vishnu himself was going to appear in this world through her womb. On the other side Kansa had also taken extra precautions against the birth of the eighth child. The guards were heavily armed and more number of guards were deployed.

As it happened, on the day of Krishna's birth it rained very heavily, storms lashed the streets and there was constant thunder and lightning. At this time Vishnu appeared in a vision to Vasudeva and said that he was coming and should be taken far away to be served from the killers hired by Kansa. Miraculously the prison doors opened on their own and the guards at the gate fell asleep. Vasudeva carried the newly born Krishna across the river Yamuna to the other bank. This child was also brought to the house of Vasudeva's friend Nand. He and his wife Yashoda welcomed the child to their own household. At the same time to hoodwink Kansa the child born to Nand and Yashoda was brought back to the prison by Vasudeva. Kansa did not spare the substitute child, even though it was a girl, contrary to the predictions..

Then onwards Nand and Yashoda became Krishna's foster parents. In many of the pictures Yashoda is seen holding Krishna in her arms and caressing him while in others she is seen scolding him for his mischievous pranks. Thousands of songs on the child-like plays of Lord Krishna have been composed and are being sung throughout India. People preserve at home child Krishna's image in stone, brass or other metal and worship it every morning.

The legend says that when the news of the birth of a son to Nand and Yashoda spread in the town of Gokul, a stream of people reached their house. They welcomed the arrival of the new child by singing and dancing. Mother Yashoda crooned over her son. She rocked her son in his cradle just as Hindu women through so many centuries have continued to rock Lord Krishna on the day of his birth, known as Janmashtami. The customary worship today is done by putting a cucumber in the cradle, which represents the birth of infant Krishna.

When Nand got the child's horoscope cast, the learned Brahmans declared that the child was destined to do great deeds and that he would destroy so many demons. The fascinating tale of the infancy days of Lord Krishna comprise of his baby pranks, his capacity for mischief, the immense affection of his foster-mother, Yashoda, the endless love of the cowgirls for this child and also of his supernatural powers at this age. Time after time Krishna protected the cowherds from harm and defeated the forces of evil. In this way Krishna passed his early life-the life of a god born amidst the simple village folk.

Putana was the first demoness who tried to kill Krishna. She killed small children by breast-feeding them. This demoness assumed the form of a beautiful girl and came to Yashoda's house. Enchanted by her fake beauty Yashoda allowed Putana to hold the baby and then to suckle him. Krishna fastened his tiny mouth to her breast sucking her very life out alongwith the milk. Putana tried to push the child away but to no avail. This way the demon met her end and Yashoda found the child safe and sound sucking her breast. At the time of her death Putana regained her ugly demoniacal shape. The second attack on Krishna came from another demon, Shaktasura (a demon in the form of a wooden cart) who was also defeated and killed by Krishna.

When Krishna became five months old, he was attacked by Trinavartta, the demon of storm and whirlwind. The demon seized child Krishna and whirled him into the air. Yashoda and other cowgirls alongwith other men-folk searched the child everywhere in panic, but the child had forced the demon down and dashed him to death against a rock. After a while the searching team discovered Krishna playing on the chest of the dead demon. They were filled with great joy and Yashoda picked the child and hugged him to her bosom.

A sage was summoned to name the two children of Vasudeva, brought from Mathura to Gokul-one nurtured by Rohini, the first wife of Vasudeva and the other fostered by Yashoda, the wife of Nand. The sage named the two children Balarama and Krishna. Balarama was also given six other names but the sage declared that Krishna, being born in Vasudeva's house, was to be called Vaasudeva though his names were numberless as he was the incarnation of God and had been born to remove the ills of the world. The sage said that the other child too was a part of Vishnu and was the incarnation of Sheshanaga. Thus they learnt about the true character of both the children but preferred to remain silent and continued treating Krishna as their son.

Both the brothers grew up at Gokul. When Krishna started walking he indulged in his naughty pranks like stealthily entering the houses of cowgirls and stealing the cream, curd and butter made and stored by them. Though Krishna was sometimes caught by them yet by his innocent talks he always outwitted them and they went back bursting into laughter. Once Yashoda became very angry and tied him to a mortar. After a while Yashoda heard a loud crash and when she came running she found that Krishna had dragged the mortar between the trunks of two trees, pulled them down and was quietly sitting between them. Legends hold the view that, two young men by the names of Kuvera and Nala had been imprisoned in these two trees and Lord Krishna had released them by this action.

By this time Nand and Yashoda left Gokul and got settled in a forest region called Brindaban. Krishna was now five years old. A demon named Vatsasura turned himself into a cow and mingled with the herd. His presence was recognised by Krishna, who seized the demon-cow by the hind legs, whirled it round his head and dashed it to the ground. He was then confronted by another demon, Bakasura, who attacked Krishna in the form of a crane. This huge bird opened its peak and engulfed Krishna. The incarnate Lord tore its beak into two and came out. Krishna was later on attacked by a snake-demon, Ugrasura which swallowed the Lord. At this Krishna expanded his body to such an extent that the snake burst into tiny bits.

At the age of eight, Krishna did another amazing feat. Krishna alongwith his friends reached the banks of, river Yamuna to play. In the river there was a dangerous whirlpool, in which lived the giant snake, named Kaliya. The Lord and his cowherds started playing ball. A solitary Kadam tree stood by the bank and Krishna climbed it. One cowherd threw the ball towards Krishna but it fell into the river. Krishna plunged into the river to bring out the ball. Kaliya, the snake, detected that a young boy had entered his domain. It began to spout poisonous substance and encircled Krishna in its coils. Nand, Yashoda and others were greatly alarmed to hear this and rushed to the bank of the river. Yashoda in agony was about to jump into the river when Krishna came upon the surface of the water playing his flute as he stood upon the head of Kaliya. He had subdued the mighty snake with his superhuman strength.

Another phase of Krishna's life at this stage is the mad love of cowgirls for this charming boy. As Krishna grew up, his charm exuded love and he attracted everybody. Even the married cowgirls found his beauty irresistible. Playing on his flute Krishna enchanted these girls. In the later centuries, probably during the tenth and twelfth century, account of a cowherd girl named Radha came into great prominence as the constant lover and companion of Krishna. She was the daughter of Vrishabhanu and was married to Ayaan. This woman fell madly in love with Krishna and became immortal. Now her image can be seen at the side of Krishna in almost all the temples. In all the stories of Krishna's youth Radha is given the most prominent place and in the famous Raas-lila dances she is the main figure. Radha is invariably shown dancing together with Krishna while all other cowgirls are only seen moving in circle around the two. These days this episode is given a philosophical meaning, that Radha represents the soul while Krishna represents God. Thus Radha's love means yearning of the soul for merger with the Almighty.

Amongst the other exploits of Krishna during those days is one concerning Indra, a very powerful god during the early vedic period but later reduced to the status of a chief of smaller gods. Jealous of Krishna's fame, Indra being the king of skies, called upon clouds to rain down in torrents at Brindaban. Scared by the unbearable downpour from above, the cowherds and other people of the region appealed to Krishna for relief. Krishna calmed their fears and raised the Govardhana hill overhead with support of his little finger. Indra kept on pouring torrential rains for seven days but Brajbhumi's people remained dry under the shelter of the Govardhana hill. Indra was compelled to relent and admitted that in the incarnation of Krishna, Lord Vishnu had himself appeared on the earth. Later he was forgiven for his rashness and he returned to his kingdom of heavens.

Notwithstanding all these pranks, feats and frivolous deeds of Krishna, the real reason for his birth was that of ridding this earth of the vicious tyrant Kansa. This king in his search for the child, who was destined to kill him, slaughtered many children. Krishna was also subjected to a number of attacks but he survived each of them with his supernatural powers. One day, however, a sage disclosed to Kansa that his true enemy was alive. Kansa in consultation with his counsellors hatched a plot to decoy both the brothers, Balarama and Krishna, to Mathura. A special festival of armed combat was proclaimed. They anticipated that the two brothers would be coming with other cowherds to participate in the combat and that they can be killed by the wrestlers of the king. Kansa sent for Akrura, the chief of Yadavas and a leading member of his court. He briefed Akrura about his intentions. Akrura was a good man and he readily agreed to go and invite Krishna, overjoyed at the thought of meeting the Lord. He reached Brindaban and revealed to Krishna the intentions of Kansa. Krishna agreed to accompany him to Mathura together with his brother Balarama.

When Krishna and Balarama reached Mathura with Akrura, the whole city thronged the precincts of the palace to have a look at the two brothers, whose reputation had reached much in advance to this city of Mathura. Kansa had fixed the next day for the commencement of the wrestling match and the other feats of strength.

The arena for the competition was richly decorated and citizens from Mathura and nearby villages thronged the place to witness the events. Krishna's access into the arena was detained by stationing a ferocious elephant at the gate. Krishna killed the beast and entered the arena carrying the tusks in the hands. King Kansa conveyed to the two brothers that as he had heard tales of their valour, he wanted to witness their feats. The two mighty wrestlers of the court, named Chanura and Mushtika were let loose against the two brothers. In the match the two giants were badly defeated and likewise the brothers killed a few other fighters of king Kansa.

After watching this grand show all danced with joy while Kansa felt very much afraid. In rage Kansa shouted, "Kill these two sons of Vasudeva and their father. Also put to death those who have sided with my enemies." Lord Krishna jumped on to the dais where Kansa was sitting, caught him by the hair and dragged him down. In the battle between the two, Kansa was killed. Then the eight, younger brothers of Kansa attacked Krishna but they were slain by Balarama. After this Vasudeva and Devaki were released from the prison and they were filled with joy when they met their victorious sons. Lord Krishna then touched the feet of their foster father and mother, Nand and Yashoda. He said, "You two have done much more than what real parents could do." He gave them the best of presents and bade farewell to them. This way the first part of Lord Krishna's life come to an end.

The second part of the life of Krishna appears in the context of the Great War between Kauravas and Pandavas, the princes of Hastinapur. Pandavas were the first cousin of Krishna. On hearing the news of the death of Pandu, the husband of his father's sister, Krishna approached Akrura and said to him, " It is learnt that after the death of their father, king Pandu, the five brothers, Yudhishthira, Bhima, Arjuna, Nakula and Sahdeva are living together with their mother, my aunt Kunti, in the palace of king Dhritarashtra of Hastinapur. Please go there and inquire about their welfare. I have heard that the blind king Dhritarashtra is under the influence of his sons and is not treating the sons of his brother in a fair manner." From here onwards the life of Lord Krishna is interwoven with that of the history of Pandavas. Coming to the Mahabharata we find Krishna's life and actions in a different light.

During the second part of Krishna's life many minor and personal incidents occur. The slain king of Mathura, Kansa, had married two daughters of Jarasandha, the mighty ruler of Magadha. After the death of Kansa, the widowed queens went to Jarasandha and informed him of the tragedy. He with his a big army invaded Mathura. Krishna and Balarama along with their soldiers met their foe. The army of Jarasandha was defeated though Krishna spared his life. The whole city welcomed the two brothers with great joy. Krishna thereafter built a strong fortress and erected walls on all side for the protection of Mathura.

At that time the ruler of Vidarbha was Bhishmaka, who had a daughter named Rukmini. This beautiful princess after hearing the adventurous stories of Krishna had fallen in love with him. But the elder brother of Rukmini wanted to marry off his sister to Shishupala, the king of Chedi. The princess secretly sent a letter to Krishna through an emissary. In this letter she requested him to come and save her. Krishna also learnt from this emissary the day when the princess was to be married to Shishupala. On the appointed day the intended bridegroom entered the city with great pomp and show. The poor princess Rukmini felt disappointed when she found that Krishna had not reached on time to rescue her. When she had lost all hopes the emissary stealthily entered Rukmini's apartments and informed her about the arrival of Krishna together with his brother, Balarama.

In the morning Rukmini, with her escorts, proceeded towards the temple of Ambika for prayers. Krishna on his chariot was waiting on one side. He with a sudden and swift move took her on the chariot by his side and rushed towards Dwaraka. The chiefs who had assembled for the wedding gave a hot pursuit but Krishna and Balarama together with other Yadava tribe chiefs conferred on them a crushing defeat. Lord Krishna entered Dwaraka with Rukmini, and both of them got married formally. Though there are legends about sixteen thousand wives of Krishna, Mahabharata speaks of only one other wife, named Satyabhama.

In the epic of Mahabharata, Krishna appears first in the Swayamavara (marriage ceremony) of Draupadi, the daughter of king Drupada of the State of Panchal. The stage was set at Panchal for the marriage of princess Draupadi. Royal princes had come from far and near to win the hand of this beautiful princess. King Drupad declared that he would give his daughter in marriage, to the prince who is able to hit the set target with his arrow. The five Pandava brothers also entered the arena. None could hit the mark while Arjuna succeeded in hitting the mark. At this victory feat of Arjuna, the princes who had assembled there felt humiliated and became ready to fight with Arjuna and his brothers. Here Krishna interfered and persuaded the assembly not to indulge in any unjust action. He succeeded in pacifying the angry contenders. Draupadi was eventually married to all the five brothers, who in those days were living under the guise of Brahmanas.

After Draupadi's marriage, Krishna is seen as taking active part in the marriage of Subhadra, his sister. Arjuna loved her and wanted to marry her. Arjuna, after consultation with Krishna, carried away Subhadra in his chariot as other family members were opposed to this alliance.

During this period the pandavas were leading an exiled life. After sometimes Yudhishthira with his four Pandava brothers came out of their disguise and started ruling over their kingdom. But, the sovereignty of Pandava brothers could not remain unchallenged unless Jarasandha, the mighty and cruel king of Magadha, was subdued. Jarasandha had got numerous princes as his captive. Krishna challenged Jarasandha and killed him in the fight. He thus fortified the supremacy of the Pandavas and also relieved people of an oppressive ruler.

Now Yudhishthira arranged for a big Yajna (sacrificial ceremony), in which all the rajas were duly invited. Here the Pandava brothers gave the first place of honour to Krishna. This was highly resented by Shishupala, the king of Chedi State. He abused Krishna and used filthy languages against him. In the fight that ensued Krishna killed Shishupala. According to legends Krishna beheaded Shishupala with his Sudarshana Chakra (Divine wheel).

At the success of this sacrificial ceremony, Pandavas' first cousin, Duryodhana, son of Dhritarashtra (the uncle of Pandava princes), grew jealous. He challenged the Pandava brothers to a game of dice. Shakuni, the maternal uncle of Duryodhana, was the villain of the piece and he was the master of all these deceitful manouverings. As the game proceeded, Yudhishthira became more and more engrossed in it and played heavier and heavier stakes. At each succeeding loss he became desperate and after losing his kingdom and brothers, he even put his wife Draupadi at stake. When he lost her too, the evil winners wanted to dishonour her, but Krishna intervened and saved her honour. As per mythological accounts, he saved her with his miraculous powers. However as a result of this defeat and as per conditions laid down in one stake, the five Pandava brothers had to leave the kingdom and remain in exile for thirteen years.

Eventually Pandavas after completion of their exile requested for the return of their kingdom. Krishna tried his best to avoid the war by acting as envoy on behalf of Pandavas. Kauravas under Duryodhana refused to budge an inch. In this great War of Mahabharata, Krishna acted as the charioteer of Arjuna. In fact Krishna had offered both the sides a choice. Each side was given the choice of either having him as an adviser who would not actively engage himself in the battle or of having his army men as fighters in the field. Kauravas chose his army men while Pandavas opted for Lord Krishna. (It was in the capacity as a charioteer of Arjuna, that Lord Krishna recited to Arjuna the world-famous divine song of Bhagvad Gita). Thus preparations for the big war began, allies were formed and many battles followed.

The army of Kauravas was commanded in succession by their great-uncle Bhishma, their teacher Drona, their military preceptor, the half-brother of Pandavas Karna, and the King of Madra, Shalya. All the warriors fell in succession and at length Bhima and Duryodhana fought in single combat with their mace. Duryodhana had his thigh broken and was mortally wounded. At the end of this war there remained alive only the five Pandava brothers. After a reconciliation with Dhritarashtra, the blind father of the Kauravas, Yudhishthira was crowned the King. However he was greatly depressed and highly troubled at the loss of all his kith and kin. After his coronation the horse-sacrifice ceremony was performed by Yudhishthira. Later on the Pandava brothers too left the kingdom and retired to the Himalayas.

In this context what interests us regarding Lord Krishna is his divine message to Arjuna. In Bhagvad Gita, Krishna points out that to a warrior nothing is nobler than a righteous war and declares that one should do his duty without any attachment for results. He explains to Arjuna the three noble paths. First is that of Yoga (knowledge) which means yoking mind and body to achieve perfect unity beyond the limits of thought and language; second is that of Dharma (righteousness), which means religious duties and customs, while the third is that of Bhakti (devotion). Devotion implies love to a personal God and complete surrender to Him. This is the path that commands the strongest approval of Krishna. He says "Have your mind in Me, be devoted to Me, to Me shall you come.... Though I am the unborn, the changeless Self... to save the good and destroy evil doers, to establish the right, I am born from time to time."

Numerous heroic incidents happened before Krishna left the human body and returned to his heavenly abode. Legend says that the gods, headed by Brahma and Shiva approached Krishna begging him to return as the latter's mission on earth had been completed. Krishna promised the gods that within seven nights he would complete the destruction of Yadavas and return to his perennial home. Bad omens started appearing in Dwaraka; strong hurricanes, screaming birds, wailing cats and dogs, howling jackals and headless spirits drew the attention of all Yadavas in Dwaraka. Krishna advised the residents to leave Dwaraka and move to Prabhasha, a site further inland. Krishna had now made last preparations for their annihilation. On the way the Yadavas drank heavily and struck one another with fatal blows. In a short time no Yadava was left alive except mighty Krishna and Daruka, his charioteer. Only those left behind at Dwaraka were spared to continue the race of this tribe. Balarama, the brother and companion of Krishna, went to the seashore, performed yoga and left his body returning to his real self, viz., Sheshanaga, the serpent of eternity. Once when Krishna was sitting under a fig tree in a yogic posture a poisonous arrow by a hunter, mistakenly struck the sole of his left leg which served as a prelude for his final departure. He instructed Daruka, his charioteer, to go to Dwaraka and break the news to the residents about his end. Finally the ocean came up and swallowed the city of Dwaraka engulfing everything except the temple.

The entire legend of Krishna's life and his leelas (deeds) provide a great opportunity for presentation of those events through architecture, poetry, music and dancing. The many facets of his endearing activities have fired the imagination of people, which no other incarnation has done. He is a naughty boy, a romantic lover, a heroic warrior, a shrewd diplomat and a great 'Sanyasi' (ascetic). He is not only the pivotal character of an epic but also the author of one of the most sacred books of the Hindus-a treasure house of philosophy and a fountain of solace to the troubled hearts. It has been said that in Krishna we have the fullest and the most perfect manifestation of the Divine.

NARASIMHA

Narasimha, the fourth incarnation of god Vishnu, is half-lion half-human and provides a very fascinating study of Lord's incarnation in order to alleviate the sufferings of devotees. This story is also very interesting.

Among the descendants of Daksha (the first man created by Brahma), there was one Kashyapa, a sage, who had four wives, Diti, Aditi Vinata and Kandru. Diti gave birth to demons and from Aditi were born gods, while from Vinata was born Garuda, the carrier of Vishnu and the last one Kandru created the hydras.

Out of the demons born of Diti, two possessed terrific powers. These two brothers were named Hiranyaksha and Hiranyakashipu. Both of them performed so many religious practices and austerities that in course of time they gained unlimited powers. Brahma was so pleased with their penances that he bestowed on Hiranyakashipu the priceless boon of immortality. He was blessed in such a manner that he cannot be destroyed by a common human being or animal or god born in the natural process, nor can he die during day or night, neither in earth nor in heaven and no weapon, water or fire can kill him.

This blessing puffed up their pride and the two demons crossed all bounds, practised all sorts of oppression and even dethroned Indra, the king of heavens. Indra in the company of all the gods appeared before Brahma and prayed for deliverance. Brahma was very much worried and replied that the two demons had become powerful due to the blessings bestowed by him on them and revealcd his inability to destroy them. He also advised Indra to approach Vishnu, which they did. These gods retold their story of sufferings to Vishnu for a solution, and said that due to the boons given by Brahma the two demons had been indulging in all sorts of oppression. Vishnu promised to destroy them in due course of time.

Hiranyakashipu had a son named Prahlada. This boy right from his very childhood was attracted towards Vishnu and other gods. Prahlada did not obey the orders of his father, not to worship Vishnu. In fits of anger at his son's disobedience, Hiranyakashipu tried to destroy his son Prahlada many a times, employing various cruel methods. Once Prahlada was tied to a stone and was thrown into the river but Vishnu himself came and saved him from drowning and dying. Hiranyakashipu later tried to get Prahlada trampled under the feet of an elephant but the elephant lifted Prahlada lovingly, with his trunk and put him on its back. Hiranyakashipu then built a house, put Prahlada into it and set the house on fire; even this could not harm Prahlada. The father even tried to poison the son but to no avail.

At last one day he shouted and asked Prahlada, "You repeat Vishnu's name day in and day out; where does this god live?" Prahlada replied mildly that He was present everywhere. The father asked, "Is that Vishnu present in this pillar also?" Prahlada replied, "Yes, very much". Hiranyakashipu shouted, "See, I will kill him then". He gave the pillar a heavy blow with his mace and surprisingly the brick-pillar burst open and Vishnu, in the form of a being-half-man and half-lion came out of it. This was Vishnu's reincarnation as Narasimha.

The shape of this god incarnate was neither of a man nor of a god nor of an animal. This god was not born from the womb in ordinary course. The time of appearance was also evening when it was neither day nor night. The demon was bodily lifted and placed by Narasimha on his knees, which was between the earth and the sky. The god tore the demon's body with his claws, thus using no weapon of any kind. This way the blessings of Brahma were not overruled. After killing Hiranyakashipu, Narasimha also killed his other demon brother.

Prahlada was in tears and asked Narasimha about the fate of his father in the after-life. Vishnu assured the devotee that as He, the Lord himself had killed the father, the latter would surely go to heaven. Vishnu also gave a blessing to Prahlada that from then onwards none of his race would die at the hands of Vishnu.

KARTTIKEYA

Karttikeya generally represented with a single face, is believed to be having six faces. Karttikeya is yellow-skinned; rides on a peacock; holds in his right hand an arrow and in his left a bow. He is widely known as the god of war. This god is also known by other names like Skanda, Kumara, Mahasena, Guha, Agnibhu, Tarakajit, Shakti, Dhuru, etc.. In southern India he is known as Subrahmanya.

In the epics, Mahabharata and Ramayana, this god is described as the son of Shiva or Rudra. Sometimes his motherhood is ascribed to Ganga (hence Ganga-putra), and sometimes to goddess Parvati, the consort of Shiva. In some legends he is said to have been born without the intervention of woman through fire (hence the name Agnibhu). This god is depicted sitting near the Shiva-Linga together with Nandi, the mount of Shiva.

The story of his birth is narrated in Kumara Sambhava. Unable to bear the torments of demon Taraka, all the gods under the leadership of Indra, went to the Creator to seek his help to get rid of this monster. The Creator advised them that only the seed of Shiva could produce a fighter, who can defeat the demon. At that time Shiva was lost in deep meditation and even the god of lust, named Kama, could not awaken

Lord Karttikeya

Lord Karttikeya — god of war and the slayer of demon Taraka.

this god. Then the goddess Parvati, came forward to help the gods. Once Shiva's passions were aroused none could bear the energy of his seed. Agni who alone could bear it, took the seed into its mouth and thereafter transferred this seed to Ganga. God Karttikeya so born is therefore called, Gangaja or Agnibhu. As he got conceived in this manner he is also called Kumar-for ever young and chaste.

Another myth connected with his birth states that the gods appealed to Shiva for help in repelling the attack of the demons. Shiva responded and assumed six faces, each with a central eye from which six sparks sprang forward. These sparks fell into a lake said to be situated some fifty miles northwest of Madras. These sparks were transformed into six infants, nursed by the six mothers who comprise the Pleiades, the six Krittikas. Shiva's wife Parvati took the six infants into her arms. She hugged them affectionately but in the process squeezed the six children so strongly that they turned into one single body with six heads. Since he was reared by the six Pleiades (Krittikas), he is popularly known by the name-Karttikeya. He was made the Lord of war and the chief of god's army. According to Mahabharata he defeated the demons Mahisha and Tara.

Legendary stories have much to say about Karttikeya's immense strength. Once, as a boy, he thrust his spear into the ground and challenged that nobody could pull it out or even shake it. God Vishnu held the lance and moved it a bit with his left hand, the result was disastrous- the whole earth-the seas, the forest, the mountains started shaking badly. Even Prahlada the strong and powerful son of Hiranyakashipu, who was the beloved of Vishnu, could not move it a bit and fainted while attempting the feat.

It seems that during ancient times the worship of Karttikeya was much more widespread. Patanjali mentions about his images in homes and temples. The coins of Kushan kings bear his name and under the Gupta kings he was worshipped in the whole of northern India. He was also the favourite deity of the kings of Chalukya dynasty. In southern India he is still widely worshipped. Several deities of the south are associated with him, e.g., Murugan (the chaste boy), Velan (the spear-bearer) and Seyon (the red-one). His story is related in Mahabharata, Shiva Purana and Kalidasa's Kumara Sambhava. Kumar is shown riding a peacock (the killer of serpents).

A complementary story connected with his birth, is about the burning of Kama—the god of sex and lust. As mentioned earlier, the gods in order to awaken the sexual desire in Lord Shiva, assigned this job to Kamadeva. Kamadeva was highly flattered by all gods and he boasted that he could conquer the mind of Shiva within no time. Kama discussed the plan with his wife Rati, who reproved him for this temerity but later consented to accompany him and help him in disturbing Shiva's meditation. They set off together with Vasanta (spring season's god) to Himalayas. Kamadeva sent an arrow towards Shiva. The great Lord, smitten thus, awoke from meditation and shouted angrily for having dared to interrupt his meditation. When he looked towards south he spotted Kamadeva. In anger Shiva opened his third eye in the centre of his forehead and reduced Kama to ashes. Later on, responding to the pleas of his widow, Rati, Lord Shiva restored Kama to life but only as a mental being, representing true love and affection and not just physical lust. Hence the other name of Kamadeva is Ananga (the bodiless).

On the last evening of the month of Kartik, the clay image of god Karttikeya is worshipped and then submerged into the river the next day. At every great festival associated with the mother goddess Durga, his image is also made and set up by her side. Many people, especially women worship this god to beget a male offspring.

Karttikeya is sometimes referred to as Kumara or 'boy' because of his youthful appearance and unmarried status. The worship of the boy-god 'Kaumara' was once prevalent in North India, but now it is extinct. Children are not allowed to worship at his shrine. In eastern India he is worshipped once a year chiefly by immoral women. In Bombay he is considered as an inauspicious deity and married women desist from entering his shrine.

In South India he is widely revered as Murugan, who is associated with serpent worship. Now-a-days his devotees visit, his shrine especially at Palani near Madura, bearing an ornamental bamboo pole called kavadi which are hung with small pots containing milk, sugar, honey, flowers and fruit.

It is believed that all hill tracks are sacred to him and unwary travellers are often afflicted by him. It is said that in areas sacred to him cases of demon possession occurs frequently. There is a belief that the god Karttikeya is the inducer of sexual passion and his votaries danced in a frenzied manner in a ring and propitiated him with magical rites.

JAGANNATHA

Jagannatha, the Lord of the world, is the name given to a particular form of Vishnu or to be more accurate, that of Krishna. The image of this god has no legs and only stumps of arms; together with him are seated Krishna's brother Balarama and their sister Subhadra. The latter two images also does not have legs and hands. These three images are worshipped in the same form in all Jagannatha temples, situated mostly in eastern parts of India. But Puri, near the town of Cuttack in Orissa State, is considered to be the real abode of Lord Jagannatha and the chief centre of his worship is the great temple complex in that city. Three big statues of Krishna, Balarama and Subhadra are enshrined in this temple.

It is a great seat of pilgrimage for Hindus living in all parts of India. Thousands of people visit this place and on the occasion of two great festivals held there lakhs of Hindus throng the place, to have a glimpse of the Lord. These two festivals are the Snaana-Yatra (Bathing festival) and the Rath-yatra (Car festival), held during the months of Jaistha and Asadha respectively. In the first the images are given a bath and in the second (the more important one,), the image of Lord Jagannatha is brought out upon a chariot together with the other two images. On this day the whole area surrounding the temple looks like a sea of human

Lord Jagannath Ji

Lord Jagannatha — a form of Krishna is widely worshipped all over India and the temple dedicated to Jagannatha in Puri is a great seat of pilgrimage for Hindus.

ATUL 95

beings. The chariot is pulled by thousands of pilgrims in the streets and the crowd is so dense that sometimes people gets crushed in their attempt to touch or get near the chariot. The word 'Juggernaut' in English language denotes this festival as the source of its derivation and describes the character of this festival.

The origin of these statues is in itself legendary. As mentioned in the section dealing with the life of Lord Krishna, he was killed by a hunter. After sometimes some people found his remains and put them in a box. Once Lord Vishnu directed king Indradyumna to form the image of Jagannatha and put into its belly these remains of Krishna and that by doing so, the king would achieve his salvation. The king had no idea whom to approach to make such an image so he prayed to god who commanded him to pray to Vishvakarman, the personification of the creative power and the great architect of this universe. Vishvakarman undertook the assignment of making this image on the specific condition that he would not be disturbed by anybody till he completed the work. When fifteen days lapsed the king could not contain his curiosity and to have a look at the image he went to Vishvakarman who burst into rage at his impertinence and went away leaving the image without hands and feet. The image had only the stumps and the king was overwhelmed with a feeling of guilt. Later on King Indradyumna as a penance prayed to Brahma who told him that the image would not be completed but he would make the image immortally famous. Brahma gave the image eyes and a soul and also acted as high priest at the time of the installation and consecration of the image of Lord Jagannatha.

All the three images are made of wood and every twelve years the old ones are buried underground in an unfrequented part of the extensive temple compound. The original image made by Vishvakarman is said to be lying somewhere in a pool near the present temple.

The two festivals of Snaana-Yatra and Ratha-Yatra are very ceremonial. During the first festival the three images are taken out and placed on a large terrace built in an open space near the temple. Here the Brahmans, surrounded by an immense concourse of spectators, bathe the god by pouring Ganga water on the head amidst the loud chanting of stotras (sacred hymns). After this the Brahmans wipe the deities dry, carry them back to the temple and then conducts the worship ceremony. At this time all the images of Jagannatha throughout the country are subjected to the same ceremonies.

About two weeks after the Snaana-Yatra, the Car festival is held. Before the god is taken out of the temple to be placed on the chariot, the elaborate rituals of worship are performed. This chariot is in the form of an imposing tapering tower of about thirty to forty cubics height. It has sixteen wheels, two horses and one coachman, all made of wood. The three images are put in an elevated part of the carriage. The chariot is drawn by a large crowd of people who loudly chants the name of the Lord in great fervour and enthusiasm. When the chariot arrives at the specific spot the three images are taken out and kept at a place prepared for them where they remain for eight days.

Lord Jagannatha's Rath-Yatra attracts huge crowds and such processions are taken out in other parts of the country too on the same day.

Lord Suryadevji

The sun god, manifestation of the divine energy of heaven.

SURYA (The Sun)

In ancient India during the Vedic age and even afterwards Surya played a very significant role in Hindu mythology and amongst Hindu gods. Surya is one of the three chief gods in the Vedas. As one of the spheres, the physical sun is the celestial form of fire or Agni, and the source of all life. Surya is at the centre of the spheres. Above it is the unmanifest sphere of the Supreme Ruler and below it are the manifest spheres of the moon and the earth. The other name of Surya is Savitri, which means brilliance. In the later ages, like many other Vedic gods, this god became more or less a mythical figure superseded by Vishnu, who came to be regarded by Hindus as the supreme manifestation of the Self-Existent—the Supreme God.

Not withstanding all this the most celebrated mantra (hymn), known as Gayatri mantra, is the incantation addressed to Surya. Also many of the forms of meditation, prayers and rituals used in the daily ceremonies of Hindu Brahmans are meant to be addressed to this god. Daily in the morning one can see hundreds of Hindus offering water to the rising sun, accompanied with incantations. Women can be seen frequently taking a pledge that in case Surya bestows them with a son, they would be regularly performing certain ceremonies to worship this god. A legend states that about three hundred years ago a learned Hindu, who was suffering from leprosy, prayed to Surya for cure. He was inspired to write eight verses in Sanskrit, known as Suryashataka, to please the god, and by the time he had finished the last verse he was restored to health. Worship of the Surya is performed by standing towards the sun with clasped hands and closed eyes. The origin of this method of obtaining relief from sickness is ascribed to Shumbha, the son of Krishna, who was directed in a dream to repeat the twenty-one names of Surya twice a day standing in this manner.

Surya has two wives, Suvarna and Chhaya. The former is the daughter of Vishvakarman who after her marriage found that she could not bear the power of the Sun's rays. She, therefore, made an image of her own, imparted life to it and left it with Surya. Later on she was turned into a mare and adopted by Surya again.

The abode of this god is known as Suryaloka. A powerful race of Hindu kings has always taken pride in calling themselves as the direct descendants of Surya. In this dynasty of Surya vanshis the first king was Ikshvaku while god Rama was the sixty sixth king in this lineage. Even till medieval ages and thereafter so many Rajput kings claimed themselves to be the descendents of Surya.

Surya has several sons. The lawgiver, Manu; the lord of death, Yama and the river Yamuna were born of Suvarna. According to Mahabharata, the great warrior Karna was Surya's illegitimate son born to Kunti, the mother of Pandavas. Surya is also the father of the monkey chief, Sugriva, who was the ally of Lord Rama.

Chhandogya Upanishad says that at the time of creation the world's egg divided itself into two parts, one silver and the other golden. The silver part became the earth and the golden part the sky. The outer cover of the egg became the mountain; the inner cover the clouds and snow; the inside veins became the rivers and the liquid in the egg became the ocean. When the sun appeared there was a great cry from which all the beings and all their pleasures were born. Hence at his rising and setting, cries and songs are heard; all beings and desires rise toward it. Those who worship the sun as the absolute always hear beautiful sounds and feel joyous.

The well-known horses of Surya are mentioned in Rig Veda, which says, "May Surya with its seven horses arrive". The sun sits on a lotus in his chariot of seven golden mares. Sometimes the chariot has only one horse with seven heads surrounded with rays. Surya's charioteer is Aruna (the red one), who is the wise elder brother of Garuda, the vehicle of Vishnu, and is also the deity of dawn. He stands on the chariot in front of the Sun, and his strong and vast body shelters the world from Surya's fury.

He is worshipped in various names like Procreator (Savitar), Lord-of-the-Day (Arhapati), Eye-of-the-World (Jagatchakshu), Witness-of-Deeds (Karmasakshi) or Lord-of-Seven Horses (Saptashva). Though small images or visual representations of this god can be seen in some temples of other gods, Surya has only one full-fledged temple dedicated to it. It is the famous temple of Sun God at Konark in Orissa. The structural peculiarity of this shrine is that it is built mainly of blocks of laterite without the use of mortar. The blocks are all held together by a system of poise and balance—a masterpiece of the science of architecture. In this temple the weight of one stone acts against the pressure of another, much of the stability being a matter of balance and equilibrium.

The occurrence of solar eclipse and lunar eclipse also have their interesting mythological explanation. After the Churning of the Sea, when the gods and demons began to fight for nectar, Lord Vishnu adopted the form of an enchanting lady, Mohini, and began to pour nectar down the throat of the gods. One of the demons saw through this game of Vishnu and got mingled with the gods adopting their guise. The moon-god and the sun-god realised the demon's trickery and brought it to Vishnu's attention, who hacked off his head with his Sudarshana Chakra. But by that time the demon had the nectar in his throat, so, his head and the trunk remained independently alive and came to be known as the Dragon's Head or Rahu and the Dragon's Tail or Ketu respectively. At the time of the eclipse Rahu is believed to be swallowing the moon and Ketu swallowing, the sun out of their constant animosity.

It is believed that Surya is generous to his devotees, bestowing on them wealth and wisdom, but ruthless to those who opposed him. Once he communicated the Yajur Veda to the sage Yajnavalkya. He gave the wonderful jewel syamantaka to Satrajita who rendered him praise and homage. Once Mandeha (a group of demons) tried to overpower him, but he dispersed them with his blinding light.

The sect devoted exclusively to the worship of Surya as the supreme deity and the adoration of the solar orb is known as Saura, Saurya or Saurapata. Those who are strict Saura cultists do not eat until they have seen the sun and do not eat after sunset. They brand their foreheads, arms and breasts with hot iron brands. The Padma Purana says that the dedication of prostitutes to a solar temple is the best means of attainment of paradise.

Shri Hanuman

HANUMAN

Hanuman, the well-known monkey god, is worshipped in a number of temples throughout the country. In some temples his image is set up as standing alone with a mace in the right hand whereas in some others sitting in a devotional posture before the images of Rama and Sita. He is considered to be the god of power and strength, who remained a celebate all through his life. He is worshipped as the greatest devotee of Rama, who in turn loves Hanuman the most.

Hanuman's other names are Hanumant and Pavanasut. He is the son of Vayu, the lord of winds and Anjana, the female seduced by Vayu. Alongwith Rama, Hanuman is invariably worshipped and he is the most favoured deity of wrestlers and grapplers. Tuesday is the sacred day on which lakhs of Hindus worship Hanuman and pray to him for strength and prosperity.

Hanuman's deeds of bravery and feats of valour are related in great detail in the Ramayana and also scantily in a few other religious books like Mahabharata and Agni Purana. This god is described as having a short thick neck, a round red face, sharp white fangs, a mane like Ashoka flowers, a tail like Indra's banner and the ability to expand himself to the size of a large mountain or to contract himself to the size of a minute fly.

There are a number of interesting myths about this god. Hanuman, when quite young, saw the rising sun, and thought it to be a ripe fruit, he sprang up to, seized it and put it into his mouth. All the gods and goddesses, feared that if he swallowed the sun, the whole world would perish. So, they prayed to him to spit out the sun. Hanuman agreed, and thus the world was saved from complete darkness. At the age of ten, Hanuman could lift the hills sixteen or twenty miles in circumference and throw them like stones. Once swallowed by a monster, he expanded his body and the monster had to vomit this god out.

On another occasion when one monster swallowed Hanuman, he transformed himself into a very small figure and emerged out of the monster's big ear. This incident occurred when Hanuman was on his flight to Ravana's Lanka to fulfil the job assigned by Rama. On his way to Lanka a demoness named Surasa spotted him and she felt that this monkey was going to harm her near relative, Ravana and so she swallowed Hanuman. To save himself, Hanuman started expanding his body, while she started stretching her mouth till it was a hundred leagues wide. Suddenly Hanuman shrank his body and within seconds he became thumb-sized and taking the female-demon by surprise he darted out through her right ear.

The scriptures state that "his form is as vast as a mountain and as tall as a gigantic tower. His complexion is yellow and glowing like molten gold. His face is as red as the brightest ruby; while his enormous tail spreads out to an interminable length. He stands on a lofty rock and roars like thunder. He leaps into the air and flies among the clouds with a rushing noise, while the ocean waves are roaring and splashing below." Ramayana further says, "The chief of monkey army is a perfect being, no one can equal him in learning of Shastras and in comprehending the meaning and sense of scriptures. In all sciences and in the rules of austerity, he rivals the preceptor of the gods. Moreover, he is the ninth author of grammar."

Hanuman helped Rama very loyally in his campaign against Ravana. When sent as Rama's envoy, Hanuman was given a ring to convince

Sita that he was truly her husband's messenger. He crossed the seas with a formidable leap and reached Lanka. He succeeded in meeting Sita and brought her news back to Rama.

While he was in Lanka, Ravana's guards, caught him and brought him to the demon-king's court. At Ravana's command his tail was set on fire and with his burning tail, Hanuman created great havoc in Lanka. When Rama's younger brother was lying unconscious in the battlefield, he came forward to bring the herb from Himalayas that could cure Lakshmana. In the hurry, unable to trace the magical herb, he lifted the mountain itself hill and flew back to the battlefield. The arrow that wounded Lakshmana was blessed in a way that whoever was wounded in the night with it could not recover if the cure was not applied before daylight. Hanuman knew this and was determined to bring it before the sunrise. The powerful Ravana compelled the sun to arise on the mountain at midnight. Hanuman, was enraged at this conspiracy, so he leaped up, seized the sun's chariot, placed the blazing god under his arm and held the mountain on his head. It was only after the application of the medicinal herb on the wound of Lakshmana, that Hanuman set the sun free.

Hanuman accompanied Rama on his return to Ayodhya and there Rama blessed him with perpetual youth and deathless existence. He was so much devoted to Rama and Sita that once he even tore up his chest with his claws to show that the images of Rama and his wife were always in his heart. He is one of the most popular deities amongst Hindus and his pictures can be seen in almost every Hindu home.

YAMA

Yama is the god of death and is the lord of the infernal regions visited by man after the cessation of life. He is the embodiment of the rule of law and imparts justice according to deeds. The word 'Yama' means the restrainer, it is he who keeps the mankind in check.

Yama's mount is a fierce-looking black buffalo, a form which he also adopts for himself on occasions. He has got a rope noose in one hand, with the help of which he is supposed to catch his victims and a mace in the other which represents the weapon of punishment.

He gives the final decision about the actions of the living beings whether they bear or do not bear fruits, when his messengers drag the dead before his throne. In Vedas, Yama is described as the First Ancestor and has the full distinction of a god. He is shown as having a fearful and grim appearance and he wears a glittering crown upon his head.

Yama is the son of Vivasvat, the embodiment of social morality, while his mother is Saranyu (clouds), who is the daughter of Vishvakarman, the cosmic architect. Yama's twin sister is Yamai, who has the greatest affection for her brother. Yamai later appeared on earth as river Yamuna.

Lord Yama

Lord Yama — or the 'restrainer' who keeps a check on the activities of mankind and metes out punishment accordingly, to the deeds or misdeeds committed by them.

Yama being the judge of the dead, holds a court and presides over it. He is assisted by a lesser god named Chitragupta who is supposed to keep an account of the actions of men. If the actions of the deceased in his lifetime had been wicked, he is sent to suffer in a particular part of hell, while those who perform noble deeds are sent to a part of heaven.

Yama is the regent of the south quarter and so is called Dakshinasapti. His abode is named as Yamalaya on the south side of the earth and has an interesting legend around it. Mahabharata accounts this story which states that after Brahma created the three worlds, viz., earth, heaven and Patal (the subterranean region), he felt that a place for judgement and punishment of the wicked was also to be made. He therefore asked the architect Vishvakarman to build a suitable place for this purpose. Vishvakarman prepared a magnificent palace and towards the opposite of its south door he created four pits to punish the wicked. He made three other doors which were reserved for the punishment of those who were to be judged. Brahma named this palace Sanjeevani. Brahma ordered the architect to form a vast trench around it and fill it with water, which came to be called Vaitarani. Brahma next ordered Agni (the fire god) to enter this river so that the water might boil. After death each person is obliged to swim across this Vaitarani river, which gives harmless passage to good souls but the evil ones have to suffer torments and pangs while crossing this boiling river.

This legendary place in heaven created for Yama by Vishvakarman is 800 miles in circumference. This place is free from fear of enemies and the sorrow of mind and body is non-existent here. The climate is mild and salubrious and each one is rewarded in kind according to his deeds. He who has given much in charity, receives comforts of all kinds.

To the virtuous and to the sinner Yama appears in different forms. To the virtuous he appears to be "like Vishnu with four arms, dark complexioned and lotus-like eyes. His face is charming as he wears a resplendent smile." The wicked, can behold him as a fearsome figure with "limbs appearing three hundred leagues long, eyes like deep wells, lips thin like the colour of smoke and fierce. He roars like the ocean of destruction. His hairs look like gigantic reeds, his crown a burning flame. The breath from his wide nostrils blows off the forest fires. He has long teeth. His nails are like winnowing baskets. He has a stick in hand, and is clad in skins. He has a frowning brow."

Yama has three wives, named Hemamala (Golden garland), Sushila (Good-natured one), and Vijaya (Victory). Yama has two ferocious dogs, who were born to Sarama (The Fleet-one), which is the bitch that guards the herds of Indra. These two dogs have four eyes each and very wide nostrils. They guard the road to Yama's abode, on which the dead souls have to travel fast with all possible speed. These dogs are said to be wandering about on earth, among men as Yama's messengers.

There are numerous stories regarding Yama which are scattered in religious books, especially Puranas. One of them depicts Yama in a different light and is known to almost every Hindus, which shows that Yama is not without compassion. The legendary tale of Savitri Satyavan from Mahabharata has stirred popular imagination since centuries. It relates to a noble princess named Savitri who remained faithful to her husband unto death and even beyond it.

Everything started with Savitri meeting, a beautiful young man, named Satyavan, son of an exiled and blind king who had been living in a hut like a hermit. She fell in love with this exiled prince and wanted to marry him. The astrologers of her father's court warned that Satyavan was destined to die within one year. But the princess was adamant and married him. On the fixed day Yama, the god of death, himself came on the buffalo and took possession of the soul of Satyavan. Savitiri, his wife, did not beg for his soul. She was very learned and just recited the beautiful and relevant passages concerning this god from the Holy Scriptures. Yama was pleased and asked Savitri to ask for any boon except for her husband's life. Savitri requested god Yama to give back eyesight to Satyavan's father. She still continued her prayers and the god agreed to grant another favour. Savitri asked Yama to give back to her father-in-law the kingdom he had lost and this was also granted.

Yama went away holding Satyavan's soul; Savitri too followed him. Yama agreed to grant her the third favour. Savitri replied, 'I wish to give birth to hundred sons'. Yama, in a hurry, promised this boon without giving a second thought to its implications. Savitri immediately said, "But how can I give birth to them without my husband?" Yama was caught unawares and as he could not go back on his promise, he had to give back her husband's soul.

Many such legends are existent concerning this god though the wide-spread image of this deity is that of a fearful rod-bearer bent on punishing for deeds or misdeeds committed during life.

SHANI

Shani or Saturn, is the god, of whom the superstitious and orthodox Hindus are very much afraid. In all big cities his image made of iron, painted in black with four arms and a protruding red-coloured tongue, can be seen placed in street corners. People drop coins before it, pours oil over it as an act of obeisance to it. It is done to appease this god so that no harm befalls the worshipper.

According to Jyotish Tattva "If a person is born under the planet Shani, he will be slandered, his riches dissipated, his peace destroyed and his family harmed". People in general are very much afraid of this god's displeasure, which if aroused shall lead to endless sufferings.

It is a common belief that when Shani is in the ninth stellar mansion, the most dreadful events befall mankind. When Lord Rama broke the bow of Shiva in the court of king Janaka prior to his marriage with Sita, the earth sank in many places and the water of the seven seas was in turmoil. Parsuram, very startled at the noise, immediately exclaimed, "Ah! Someone has laid hands on the of hood of Sheshanaga, the king of snakes, or fallen under the ninth mansion of Shani". When Rama found that his wife Sita had been stolen by somebody, he angrily exclaimed that the person who kidnapped her must have born when

Shani was in the ninth mansion.

The vehicle of this god is shown to be a crow, which is considered to be an unlucky bird. Shani was the son of Surya and Chhaya while another account says that he was born of Balarama and Revati. He is also named as Kruradrishti (the evil eyed one). To ward off the evil influence of this god on a person, special prayers and rituals are suggested.

It is said that the sure antidote of Saturn or Shani's evil effect is the worship of Lord Hanuman. Scriptures say that when Saturn warned Lord Hanuman about his onset for seven and half years (Saade Saati), the monkey lord accepted the challenge and allowed Saturn to have his play. When the planet dwelled on Lord Hanuman's head, the monkey lord loaded heavy rocks on his head so viciously that the planet was almost crushed. Similar agony was faced by Shani when he tried to dwell on the monkey lord's body and legs. Then the planet had to bow before Hanuman, saying that whosoever worshipped Lord Hanuman shall be beyond the evil effect of the planet Shani.

NARADA

Narada, an easily recognisable figure with a lute in one hand and a pointed and knotted tuft of hair in the centre of the otherwise clean-shave scalp, plays a subsidiary but very important role in numerous mythological stories and religious scriptures of the Hindus.

According to Mahabharata, Narada was the son of Kashyapa and his mother was one of the daughters of Daksha. Another account says that he sprang from the forehead of Brahma. According to some Puranas he frustrated the scheme of his father-in-law, Daksha, to people the earth with his five thousand sons. He advised the sons to choose the path of asceticism and not to lead a worldly life. Daksha required the help of his children in the work of creation and he became very angry at Narada for having foiled his plan. Daksha was about to curse Narada but was pacified by Brahma.

Narada figures in Mahabharata and Krishna stories as the seer who foretold the death of king Kansa at the hands of Krishna. In religious books and other legends there are numerous references to Narada, though these denote a time lag of centuries. Shankaracharya, the great Hindu philosopher of the eighth century A.D. explains this anomaly by stating that such perfected beings and gods, free from the

Sage Narada

Sage Narada — a maharishi, a renowned teacher, an inspirer of poets, counsellor of kings, messenger between gods and men and also a notorious mischief maker.

bonds of ignorance and illusion, continue to appear again and again for completion of their divine missions, assigned to them from age to age.

Narada is also known as Kapivaktra or monkey-faced because once Vishnu changed his face into that of a monkey. This episode makes an interesting study of how God curbs the Ahamkar (Pride) of even the best of seers. It mentions that once Narada's meditation could not be disturbed even by Kamadeva (the god of lust). At this victory Narada was overwhelmed by a feeling of pride, unbecoming to a seer. Vishnu decided to teach him a lesson by humbling his pride. He created an illusory kingdom and a most beautiful princess. In fact, the princess was the incarnation of Lakshmi, the consort of Vishnu. When Narada reached the territory of this king, he was told that the beautiful princess will marry the prince of her choice shortly and preparations were on for the marriage ceremony. Narada saw the beautiful princess and immediately fell in love with her. He approached Shiva to seek his advice as to how to attain the beautiful maiden. Lord Shiva led him to Vishnu saying that he should borrow the same visage as that of Vishnu, which the princess could never resist and would immediately garland Narada as her husband.

Narada went to Vishnu and requested that he be given a face as handsome as that of Vishnu so as to attract the princess. Vishnu played a trick and gave the face of a monkey to Narada. Not knowing what had happened, Narada reached the court of the King where the marriage ceremony was to take place. Many other princes had also assembled over there to solicit the hand of the princess. The princess entered the hall of marriage with a flower garland in hand. Narada was sure that, the princess would select him as the companion of life as he possessed a handsome face. But to his utter dismay and great astonishment, the princess did not even look twice at his monkey face. Suddenly Lord Vishnu also appeared in the court and the princess put the garland around his neck. It was later on that Narada saw his monkey-face in a pool of water and he became mad with rage. He cursed Vishnu proclaiming that Vishnu, during his sojourn on earth, would have to bear the pangs of his wife's forcible separation from him and only a monkey would be able to relieve him of his sufferings. Thus when Vishnu was born as Rama, Hanuman helped him to free Sita from the clutches of Ravana.

In Devi Bhagwata Purana it is mentioned that once Narada asked Vishnu the secret and nature of Maya (the illusion). Vishnu led Narada to a lake and asked him to take a bath. Narada found himself transformed into a female and inspite being a great seer he forgot his identity. He as a female started taking his life as such and married a king called Taladhvaja. He also gave birth to sons and took pride in his family. Suddenly Vishnu dispelled this illusion and brought him back to the realm of reality. Narada thereby learnt the power of Maya over man.

Narada is shown as a wandering seer always on a journey. This is the result of a curse, whereby he was condemned to lead a roaming life not staying at one place. He is reputed to have invented Vina, the principal stringed musical instrument of India and is deemed to be the leader of the celestial musicians. He is famous as a mischief-maker and in India his name symbolises a person who is always indulged in mischiefs of one sort or the other. The authorship of several hymns of Rig Veda is ascribed to him and he is the author of Naradiya-dharmashastra, a great work on law and moral conduct.

It is believed that Narada was the favourite of God. His role in the world of gods and goddesses was that of taking incarnation and giving lessons of devotion to God and of His importance. He was famous in all the three realms of the universe as the accomplice of God. Narada's main task was traversing the whole universe, while singing the praise of God.

He is the chief of the Gandharvas or heavenly musicians. He is considered to be an authority in devotional songs. He is the author of Bhaktisutra in which he has elaborated upon Bhakti or devotion. It is believed that he was under the vow that he would establish the concept of Bhakti in the minds of each and every being on the earth.

It is believed that the God executed his plans through Narada.

Legends hold the view that, it was Narada who taught Bhakti to sage Valmiki, Vyas, Shukradev, Prahlad, Dhruv and Ambarish.

Bhagvad Gita and Ramayana are the products of Narada's effort. After authoring various books sage Vyasa felt depressed and at this Narada inspired him to write an epic on Bhagvad or 'the God'. Narada told sage Vyasa that by narrating the significance of God he would receive ultimate satisfaction, peace and joy. Valmiki was also inspired by Narada as a result of which the great epic Ramayana came into existence.

It is said that he led innumerable people to the path of devotion. He helped a number of people to attain ultimate union with the God. He had been an accomplice to God Vishnu in all his avataras and most particularly to Lord Rama and Lord Krishna.

VISHVAKARMAN

According to Rig Veda, Vishvakarman is the divine architect of the whole universe. He is the personification of the creative power that welds heaven and earth together. He is the son of Brahma and is the official architect of all the palaces of gods. He is painted in white, has a club in his right hand, wears a crown, a necklace of gold, rings on his wrists and holds tools in his left hand.

All the flying chariots of the gods and all their weapons are his creation. It was Vishvakarman who built the golden city of Lanka, over which king Ravana ruled. He built the city of Dwaraka, the capital of Lord Krishna after the latter had left Mathura. It was again Vishvakarman who made the Agneyastra (the weapons throwing fairy flames) and it was he who revealed the Sthapatya Veda, or the science of mechanics and architecture. Mahabharata describes him as " The Lord of the arts, executor of a thousand handicrafts, the carpenter of the gods, the most eminent of artisans, the designer of all ornaments, on whose craft all menu subsist, and whom as a great and immortal god, they continuously worship".

According to legends, his daughter Sanjana was married to Surya, the sun. As she was not able to endure the heat and light of the sun,

Vishvakarman placed Surya upon his lathe and cut away an eighth part of his brightness. The fragments that fell on the earth due to this operation were used by Vishvakarman to form "the discus of Vishnu; the trident of Shiva; the weapon of Kuvera, the god of wealth; the lance of Karttikeya, the god of war and the weapon of all other gods".

Vishvakarman is the one who made the image of Jagannatha and left it incomplete due to an interruption. He is the god whose blessings enabled Nala, the monkey, to build the bridge over sea for Lord Rama right from the coast in the south of India to Lanka of Ravana.

According to Satapatha Brahmana, Vishvakarman performed a Sarvamedha Yajna (a universal sacrifice) in which he offered up all creatures and ultimately himself too. This process of ending the universe also became a prelude to the process of creating another new universe. In this way every sacrifice is also a repetition of that first creative act. This is the representation of the drama of the cyclic process of destruction and renewal of all cosmic life and matter.

He is the presiding deity of all craftsmen. The architects and also the factory owners perform the worship of Vishvakarman when the sun enters the Bhadrapada constellation; this ceremony is performed in front of the implements of trade or a manufacturing machine. The carpenter worships the chisel, the saw, etc., the weaver prays before the shuttle while the potter worships the wheel. On this day an atmosphere of festivity is blended with the rituals of prayers. As an independent god, Vishvakarman is still worshipped in some parts of Bengal.

THE KALKI INCARNATION

Prediction about the future events or happenings has always been a favourite endeavour of all the religious faiths. Whether it is the Resurrection or Rapture or the Kalki-Incarnation, each faith has imagined the onset of better times it is own way. This occurrence is the natural corollary to the concept that the noble values decay with the passage of time. The Hindu mind is basically rooted to the fact that the world always decays after its inception. Hence the first age, the Satyayuga, was the best period when Dharma, represented by the holy bull, stood on all the four legs. Then came the Treta age in which the moral and spiritual conditions deteriorated a bit and the Dharma lost one of its legs. By the time, the third age, Dwapara surfaced the Dharma lost its two legs. In the same sequence, the worse age is supposed to be the Kaliyuga or the present age when the Dharma-bull is standing only on one leg. In each of these ages the imbalance created by the adverse conditions was to be set right by various incarnations of the Lord Almighty (believed to be Lord Vishnu) in a variety of mortal forms. Srimad Bhagvad Gita says that the Lord incarnates Himself whenever there is decline of the noble values and wickedness takes an upper hand. These incarnations come in the mortal forms choosing their manner of entry into the world according to the demand of times. Just after the Deluge, He took the incarnation of the fish and later of the boar. Since Hiranyakashipu, the tyrant demon and father of Prahlada, was to be slain by a half-man-half-beast being, He came in the Narasimha form. Ravana was to be slain by a man so He incarnated in the form of a human being. And as it is expected, the worse the period, the more powerful would be these incarnations. That is, each passing age would demand a more potent incarnation, like that of Lord Rama in Treta, who was potentially less powerful than that of Lord Krishna in Dwapara because of the progressively growing adverse conditions.

It is said that in the present age, Kaliyuga, the moral conditions shall be touching their nadir and they would require the most potent incarnation to restore order in the world. That incarnation is believed to be the Kalki-Avatara or the Kalki incarnation.

This incarnation has been described in various ways by the sacred texts. As the future incarnation, Kalki will come at the end of the present Kaliyuga when moral excellence will no longer be existent, the rule of law will have disappeared and all will be darkness. In some texts he is described as holding a flaming sword, and in some as a four-armed being holding a sword, conch shell, wheel and an arrow, and in some others as having a human body with the head of a horse and holding all the things mentioned above but, but holding a club (gada) instead of an arrow.

The Mahabharata is more specific in its description of the Kalki-Avatara. On being asked by Yudhishthira, sage Markandeya, described the Kalki incarnation. According to him, "inspired by the Supreme Spirit, in a certain village called Shambhal, a son will be born in the house of a Brahmana named Vishnuyasha and this boy's name shall be Kalki Vishnuyasha. This Brahmana boy shall be extremely powerful, intelligent and valiant. He shall get all weapons, armies, etc., at will. He will collect a huge army of Brahmana warriors and shall go about setting order of righteousness in the world. He shall not only re-establish the rule of Dharma but shall also herald the advent of the Golden Age or the Satyayuga of the next cycle of time."

This incarnation shall also be with full potency. It is believed that a

Purnavatara or an incarnation with full potency has sixteen kalaas or phases. Five of these he shares with human beings and other animals, like the five doors of perception-sight, hearing, smell, taste and touch. Another four he shares with human beings-mind, heart, intelligence and the turyavastha or transcendence of intuitive experience. The seven phases that follow are characteristic of a 'Purnavatara', an integral or all-inclusive Avatara like the grace or reward for effort that fails to be rewarded though it has come from the deserving; anugraha or special grace whether the recipient merits it or not; the power to create a new order of life in society, new status of consciousness in individual or new objects; power to support and sustain what is inherently good, which may happen to be defenceless; the power to destroy what is evil; the assumption of a form which, whenever recalled mentally or in the presence of the Avatara himself, affording a solution to the problem that beholder has in mind; and the assumption of a 'name' which has a similar potency. Kalki Incarnation shall have all these above-mentioned powers to herald the Golden Age of peace and plenty-the Satyayuga. Since Kalki will be an age-making Avatara, he has to be that much powerful and potent.

INDRA

Indra, the god of firmament and the king of the abode of gods, is probably the most colourful character in Hindu mythology. The ebb and tide of his career, the rise and fall of his power provides a very fascinating story to all, who are interested in the lives of Hindu gods and goddesses.

In the Vedas, rather during early vedic age-Indra stands as the top-ranking figure among gods. Still he is not equivalent to Omkara or Brahma because he has a parentage. His complexion is golden and sparkling; he rides on a golden chariot drawn by two red strong horses with thick and flowing manes and pointed tails. His pet weapon is the thunderbolt, which he carries in his right hand; sometimes he is also represented as having a big bow with long pointed arrows as well as a big hook and a net, in which he is said to entrap his enemies.

He is the ruler of the atmosphere and the weathers are at his command. Whenever and wherever he thinks it proper, Indra sends rains as well as thunder and lightning. As a high-ranking god he had been shown as the preserver and rescuer of cows, priests and even gods. He once killed a demon named Vala, who had stolen cows so as to deny milk for the use of men and for religious ceremonies. In the earlier vedic period he is considered to be a great warrior, who subdued the enemies of Aryans and conquered their forts. During his warfare against enemies of gods he was assisted by other lesser gods-especially Marutas. He has got more hymns of praise than any other gods in the Vedas and he was then widely worshipped for his kindness, and as the bestower of rains and the giver of fertility. He is shown to have a beautiful consort, who is named Indrani.

In the post-vedic period and during the age of Puranas, Indra falls from the front rank status and is given the lower grade in all respects. Though still the king of other smaller gods, Indra is considered much inferior to the holy triad of Brahma, Vishnu and Shiva. He is still regarded as the controller of atmosphere, but only under the supervision of the Almighty. Indra in later ages is the ruler of only Swarga or the heaven where the gods live enjoying life in the company of beautiful apsaras, the female dancers. He is now depicted with great weakness and big faults. He is even shown as having lascivious character; indulging in sexual wrongs. It is said that he tried to seduce the pious wife of sage Gautama, named Ahilya. This enraged the sage, who cursed him with thousand wounds resembling female organ on his whole body. When he repented and prayed, these thousand wound marks were changed into thousand eyes; hence Indra is also called Sahasrachakshu (the thousand eyed).

In the Ramayana, there is a story that Ravana, the demon-king of Lanka, attacked heaven and fought against Indra. Indra was badly defeated by Ravana's son, named Meghanada, who since then was called Indrajit. As Indra was taken captive by Meghanada, other gods under the leadership of Brahma, had to purchase Indra's freedom by bestowing on the demon the blessing of an immortal life. There are a number of legendary tales which show that he is very much afraid to lose his throne of heaven and regularly sends beautiful singing and dancing girls to disturb the penances of the holy men, who Indra thinks may dethrone him.

During the time when God incarnated himself as Lord Krishna, Indra receives a good lesson. He pours incessant rain to drown the people of Brajbhumi, God Krishna raises the mountain named

Govardhana, on his little finger and defeats the design of Indra. Once when Krishna visited swarga, he insisted on carrying the divine Parijata tree, which resulted in a fight. Indra tried to oppose but Krishna defeated him and carried away the tree.

Though Indra is not the object of direct worship in temples, he constantly appears in all tales of religious scriptures as the king of lesser gods. Indra is actually a position, which the aspirant god attains if his divine conduct is beyond any blemish. According to the mythological details even a mortal being or a man can attain it. For instance, king Nahusha once got the seat of Indra. But he fell from the grace when he tried to lay hands on the previous Indra's wife. Hence whoever becomes the Indra has to guard his position by his good conduct.

Lord Agni

Lord Agni— the fire god, giver of good things and a relentless opponent of darkness and evil.

AGNI

Agni (Fire) is one of those very few gods who have retained complete, unimpaired supremacy in the Hindu hierarchy of gods right from the Vedic age till today. Agni is one of the three supreme deities of Rig Veda, namely Agni, Vayu and Surya. These three gods preside over earth, air and sky respectively.

In Rig Veda the largest number of hymns are addressed to Agni. Agni, as per scriptures, has seven tongues, each of which has a separate name and licks up butter offered in sacrifices.

Agni is the son of Angiras and the grandson of Sandili, one of the seven great sages. In the Mahabharata there is an interesting episode, where Agni is said to have exhausted his vigour by devouring too many oblations and therefore desires to consume the whole Khandava forest so as to regain his strength. He is prevented by Indra, but eventually with the help of Krishna, Agni consumes this forest.

Vishnu Purana on the other hand says that Agni is the eldest son of Brahma. His wife is Svaha and through this marriage he begot three sons—Pavaka, Pavamana and Suchi, and through them he got forty-six grandsons. Thus Agni has forty-nine members as his descendants.[1] According to Harivamsha, Agni is clothed in black and has smoke as his standard and carries a flaming javelin. He has four hands and rides in a chariot drawn by red horses.

Agni Purana is said to have been recited by Agni himself to sage Vasishtha. It has portions on ritualistic and mystic methods of worship, the art of wars, the laws of Hindus and the glorification of Shiva.

It is also believed that Agni is the personification of the three forms of fire, namely, the sun, the lightning and the sacrificial fire. He is considered to be the source of the Vedas, possessing and knowing all created things, the mediator between men and gods, the protector of men and their homes. Agni is invoked on every occasion as a witness to that particular action. During the crematory rites he is considered to be assuming a hideous form and is called Kravyad, 'flesh eating'; a rakshasa or ogre, since he consumed the flesh of men.

There are a number of epithets addressed to Agni like Abjahasta (lotus in the hand); Anala (fire); Chhagaratha (ram-charioted); Dhumaketu (soke forming); Hutasa or Hutabhuj (devourer of offerings); Jata veda (formed of the Vedas); Pavaka, Suchi or Shukra (bright); Sapta-jihva (seven tongned); Tomara-dhara (Javelin bearer); Vahni (conveyer of offerings) Vaisvanara (belonging to all men).

---

[1]Mythologically there are forty nine types of wind, and each wind is responsible for striking each of the descendents of Agni. Since wind enhances the intensity of fire, this natural phenomenon has been given a mythological interpretation.

Goddess Lakshmiji

LAKSHMI

Goddess Lakshmi in the Hindu pantheon of gods and goddesses is personified as the goddess of fortune and also as the embodiment of loveliness, grace and charm. She is depicted as seated on a lotus flower though sometimes she is also seen as standing on a lotus. In pictures, gold coins are seen dropping down from the palms of this goddess of prosperity. The story of the birth of goddess Lakshmi presents an interesting reading.

Her emergence in the world is connected with a famous episode in the Hindu myth called Samudramanthana (churning of the ocean), when with great efforts, by churning, the ocean was made to give up all its treasures and benefits to the world. The churning was a colossal affair and only by the efforts of Vishnu could this enterprise be successfully concluded. Vishnu advised gods to make peace with the danavas (demons) and enlist their co-operation in the venture. In return for his help the demons were to receive a share of the sacred amrita (ambrosia) which would emerge from the ocean and make them also immortal.

The gods chose Mount Mandra as the churning rod around which they coiled the serpent Vasuki which served as a churning rope. The gods held the tail and the demons the head while Vishnu took the shape of a tortoise (the second Avatara) to serve as the base for the churning rod, i.e., the mountain of Mandra. The churning was done the way one churns the milk to produce butter out of it, and 14 most precious articles[1] were received from the ocean by this process. They were, Surabhi, the cow of abundance, which was given to seven lower-status gods; Varuni or Sura, the goddess of wine; the celestial tree, called Parijata, which fulfils every desire, this was planted by god Indra in his garden; Rambha, the apsara (the heavenly dancer), who became the progenitor of all apsaras; Chandra (the moon), which was taken by Shiva and adorned on his head; Dhanvantari, the celestial physician with his vessels containing medicines; a container holding Amrita (Ambrosia); Kaustubha, the most precious stone, which came to the lot of Vishnu; Airavata, the winged elephant, which Indra took as his mount; Uchchhaisravas, the white horse with a black tail which was taken by Bali, the demon; Shankh, the white conch shell, which was taken by Vishnu; Visha (poison) was the most effective and fiery substance which no one except Shiva could swallow. It left a visible blue spot on his throat and for this reason Shiva is also known as Nilakantha (the blue throated Lord). At the end of the churning, emerged Lakshmi or Sri, the goddess of wealth and beauty. Sri was taken by Vishnu as his wife. This is how Lakshmi was born and became the consort of Vishnu.

As she came seated on the lotus flower, she is also called Padma. She being the most faithful companion of life, has always appeared as the life partner in every incarnation of Vishnu. When Vishnu came on earth as Vamana (the Dwarf), Lakshmi came to earth as Lotus (Padma or Kamla); when he came here as Parsuram, Lakshmi followed him as his wife Dhari, when Vishnu appeared incarnated as Rama, she came here as Sita; and when Vishnu appeared as Krishna, Lakshmi came in two forms, first as Radha and later as his wife Rukmini. Lakshmi has other names like Lokamata (World's mother); Chanchala (the fickle fortune); Jalandhija (the ocean born); and Haripriya (beloved of Vishnu).

In mythology, whenever she is associated with some part of the

---

Actually they were fourteen gems or ratnas.

body of a person it signifies different gifts. When she is staying at the feet, she bestows the gift of a house; when on the thigh, she gives wealth; when in the bosom, she gives a lucky child; when in the genitals, a very lucky wife; when on the heart, she gifts the fulfilment of wishes; when around the neck, the result is a meeting with the loved ones or with some lost relatives; and when in the face, the goddess bestows beauty and grace.

This goddess is sometimes represented with four arms but more often only with two. She has no temple exclusively set apart for her but always appears only as a consort of Vishnu. Still she is regularly worshipped in every shop and home-specially on the day of Diwali festival, she is worshipped, alongwith Ganesha in almost all Hindu business houses. Many people indulge in gambling too on that night, apparently to find out how their fortunes shall work in the coming year.

In some pictures goddess Lakshmi is also shown seated along with Vishnu on the divine eagle, Garuda. Goddess Lakshmi is invoked to earn the blessings of good things of life and if somebody suffers any loss in business, it is believed that goddess Lakshmi has left his house. Her figure is sometimes depicted on the door of homes to bring good luck and to drive away evil influences. Interestingly enough bad luck is personified in Alakshmi, the sister of Lakshmi.

In Bengal, goddess Lakshmi is depicted on earthen vessels and worshipped on the day just after the Durga Puja. A basket or a pot used as a corn measure, painted red and decorated with flowers is considered as goddess Lakshmi and worshipped and when it is filled with unhusked rice she manifests herself in the shape of seedlings grown in the winnowing basket.

Sometimes this goddess is considered to be unified with Lord Vishnu, and hence is called Lakshmi Narayana. This conjoined deity denotes that in his supreme state Vishnu is one with his consort, who represents his power and energy.

In the Vedas the term Lakshmi occurs in the sense of auspicious, and also means a fortunate woman. In the earlier legends Lakshmi is said to be the goddess of good fortune and beauty who issued from the mouth of Prajapati, and was the wife of Aditya. Certain other legends consider her as the daughter of the maharishi Bhrigu who in a fit of anger cursed all celestial beings. Lakshmi, his daughter was also one among them and she took refuge in the primeval waters. It is believed that it was from here that she reappeared during the churning of the ocean in the full bloom of her divine beauty, floating in the dew of a lotus flower. It is in the later legends that she is considered as the spouse of Vishnu.

Goddess Sarasvati

Sarasvati — the goddess of learning and knowledge and also speech.

ATUL·VARDHAN
95

SARASVATI

Sarasvati, the goddess of learning and knowledge, is the wife of Brahma, the creator of the world. She is represented as an extremely beautiful woman with milk-white complexion, sitting or standing on a water lily and playing on a lute.

She presides over and protects every form of art and is credited with the invention of writing. On the fifth day of the expanding moon, fortnight during the month of Magha, the worship of this goddess is performed. Either her image or even a vessel with pen, an inkstand and a book is worshipped. These articles are supposed to form a proper substitute for the goddess, who is also named as Vagvadini, the deity of eloquence. Offerings are placed with flowers on these objects and prayers are chanted from scriptures.

She is also the goddess of speech, the power through which knowledge expresses itself in action. In the Vedas, Sarasvati is primarily a river but in the hymns she is celebrated both as a river and deity. This sacred river, although now dried up, is referred to in the Rig Veda as "she who goes pure from the mountains as far as the sea". According to Mahabharata, the river was dried up by the curse of the sage Utathya. As a river, Sarasvati received great laudations for her fertilising and purifying powers. This river was once known as the giver of fertility and wealth.

Though Rig Veda does not specifically mention her as Vach, the goddess of speech, but she is clearly bestowed with this status in Mahabharata and Brahmanas. Dr. Muir attempts to explain the acquisition of this character by Sarasvati in these words, "When once the river Sarasvati had acquired the divine character, it was but natural that this river should be regarded as the protector and patron of the rituals and that ceremonies accompanied by hymns be performed at her banks. For this purpose the blessings of Sarasvati would have been invoked for their proper and successful performance... This idea must have been further extended to the very composition of these hymns... All this must have resulted in identifying Sarasvati with Vach, the goddess of speech."

On the day consecrated to Sarasvati, the musical instruments in the house are cleansed, placed on an altar and devotedly worshipped, these being the abode of this goddess.

GAYATRI

Gayatri is in fact the name applied to one of the most well known Vedic hymn consisting of twenty-four syllables. This hymn is addressed to god Surya (sun) as the supreme generative force. Being translated this hymn means -"We meditate on that glorious light of the divine Surya (Sun), may he, the lord of light, illuminate our minds." It is ordained that repeating this hymn again and again leads to salvation. One who desires to attain heaven recites it a thousand times each day. A man of the upper caste, who daily repeats the Gayatri hymn 3000 times in a month shall be freed from guilt, however great.

Gayatri later came to be personified as a goddess. She is shown as having five heads and is usually seated within a lotus. She is another consort of Brahma. According to the myth, once while Brahma was performing a sacrificial ceremony, Sarasvati did not reach there at the specified time. Brahma became very angry because her consort's presence was indispensable to complete the ceremonies. Brahma asked the priest to fetch him any woman and wed him to her at the spot. Just in the neighbourhood he found a very lovely shepherdess. In reality she was none other than the Vedic hymn of Gayatri incarnated in the form of a beautiful girl. Brahma immediately married this girl and kept her as his second wife.

The five heads of Gayatri represent the four Vedas of ancient Aryans and the remaining one represents the Almightly Lord himself. In her ten hands she holds all the symbols of Lord Vishnu including mace, lotus, axe, conch, sudarshana chakra, lotus, etc. One of the sacred texts explicitly reads: "The Gayatri is Brahma, the Gayatri is Vishnu, the Gayatri is Shiva, the Gayatri is Vedas."

The importance of Gayatri Mantra[1] is accepted by all sects of Hindus. Even the Arya Samajists, who do not believe in the worship of images and idols, proclaim this hymn as the most sacred one and in every prayer they repeat this holy mantra to achieve success as well as salvation.

---

[1] Om bhur bhuvah Svaha
tat Savitur varenyam
bhargo devasya dhimahi
dhiyo yonah Prachaodayat

GANGA

This goddess representing the holy river of Ganges is shown as an extremely fair woman, wearing a white crown, sitting on the sea-animal, crocodile, holding in her right hand a water lily and in her left hand a lute.

Rig Veda mentions the name of Ganga only twice but in the later period of Puranic age, Ganga assumed greater importance as a goddess. The legend says that she was produced from the sweat of Vishnu's feet, which Brahma caught and filled in his kamandala (vessel-container).

The story of Ganga's coming from heaven to earth is a famous mythological tale. Sagara, a legendary king of Ayodhya had no children. He performed long and arduous penances as a result of which he was promised with the birth of sixty thousand children. He did get these sons and when they grew up, king Sagara resolved to perform the Ashvamedha Yajna (the horse-sacrifice ritual). Indra, the lord of heavens was alarmed and he feared that Sagara would become very strong and dethrone him.

Indra descended to the earth and stealthily carried away the horse, and he placed it in patal (the subterranean region) just near the place where the famous sage Kapila was sitting in deep meditation. The sixty thousand sons of Sagara, after searching the horse all over the earth, dug a hole and reached patal. There they found the horse standing near a sage who was sitting with eyes closed in meditation. They thought that he was the thief and began beating him. Sage Kapila, who awoke from his meditation, in his anger reduced all the princes to ashes.

The wandering sage Narada informed Sagara about the fate of his sixty thousand sons. King Sagara prayed to sage Kapila for relief, who advised that if he could somehow bring the goddess Ganga from heavens to the earth and if the ashes were washed with her water, their salvation would be possible. Sagara gave the throne to his single surviving son and went to forest for prayers but perished in his efforts. So also his son, who too sacrificed his life as a penance after giving throne to his son (Sagara's great grand-son), Dalip.

For many years, no issue was born to Dalip from any of his two wives. Later with god Shiva's blessings he did get a son named Bhagiratha who was deformed. When this boy became young a sage blessed him and he turned into a healthy and handsome prince. Bhagiratha now addressed prayers regularly to different gods for the restoration of his sixty thousand relatives suffering on account of a curse. He performed severe penance and prayed earnestly for a very long time. Both god Shiva and goddess Ganga were ultimately propitiated.

As Ganga had to fall from heaven to earth, Bhagiratha feared that the earth will be crushed by her fall. So Ganga swept down in three great instalments and Shiva standing on the Himalaya, caught Ganga in his matted hair to mitigate the impact. At length Shiva allowed a part of Ganga to fall on earth and Bhagiratha blowing the conch given to him by god Vishnu led Ganga to seas. Later she was taken to patal (nether region) and so all the sixty thousand sons of Sagara were purified, restored to life and thus saved from doom.

On their way to the nether region what happened to Ganga is also not less interesting. While accompanying Bhagiratha, Ganga asked him the exact spot where his sixty thousand relatives were lying, whom she was supposed to deliver. As he could not inform her the proper location, Ganga before entering the sea divided herself into one hundred streams so as to ensure the salvation of the cursed wherever they might be lying. When Ganga was thus falling from the heaven to the earth, the gods prayed to Brahma that they also needed Ganga in the heavens to wash off their sins. At this Brahma assured them that a part of Ganga would remain in heaven too. Thus goddess Ganga is called Mandakini in heaven, Ganga on earth and Bhagirathi in patal.

This goddess bears a great importance in holy books. Puranas declare that the sight, the name and the touch of Ganga absolves one from all his sins and that bathing in Ganga bestows blessings of the highest order. Not only those who bathe in Ganga obtain swarga (heaven), but also those, whose bones, hair, etc., are left in the river. All the land over which Ganga flows is regarded as hallowed ground.

The cremation of a dead body at the banks of Ganga and throwing the remains in its water even though the dead bodies are burnt elsewhere is thought to be propitious. It is preferred that the bones of the deceased are brought to Ganga and cast into the holy river. It is said that this leads to salvation of the deceased.

A well-known mythological story concerning Ganga is given in Mahabharata. The father of mighty Bhishma, named Shantanu fell deeply in love with Ganga. She agreed to marry him on condition that he would never criticise her nor oppose any of her actions which included the killing of their children and that if he broke this condition she would immediately leave him. They both started living happily and seven sons were born to them. Ganga drowned each child that was born to them in the river. When the eighth child was born and she was ready to drown it, Shantanu forbade her. The life of this child, named Bhishma, was thus saved but Ganga left the prince and king Shantanu forever.

Hindus particularly choose this river for holy rituals because the merits of works performed here become manifold in their results. Another name of Ganga is Vishnupadi, the one flowing from the foot of god Vishnu. Vishnu Purana says that Ganga encloses Brahma's great city situated on Mount Meru and then gets divided into four mighty rivers flowing in four directions.

Gangajala, the water of Ganga, is held so sacred that with this in hand no Hindu would dare speak untruth. Those who die within the specified limits around Ganga, called Gangakshetra (the land of Ganga), are believed to go to the heavenly world and all their sins washed off.

Some other rivers considered sacred by the Hindus are Yamuna, Sarayu, Sindhu, Godavari, Kaveri, Narmada, Gomati and Brahmaputra.

Supreme Mother Goddess Durga

Goddess Durga — renowned slayer of demons, wife of Shiva, personifying Shakti or divine energy.

DURGA

Durga, the consort of god Shiva, is perhaps the most important goddess of Hindus. She is a multi-dimensional goddess. She has so many names, so many personalities and so many facets. She is worshipped by millions of people all over India and a sizeable number of them give more importance to her than to god Shiva himself.

She was first born in the house of Daksha, one of the progenitors of mankind and was named Sati. She was married to Shiva but sacrificed her life by self-immolation on a pyre. The story says that Daksha instituted a massive sacrifice and in the ceremonies, apportioned no share to Shiva. Sati, his daughter, had come to this ceremony against the advice of her husband, who was not invited by Daksha. Sati could not bear the insult heaped upon her husband by her father and she entered the sacrificial fire.

When Shiva heard the news he flew into rage and reached the place where Daksha was performing the sacrificial ceremony and he pierced the sacrificial altar with great violence. He ran up to the gods sitting there and knocked out all things at the spot. A number of powerful demi-gods in attendance to Shiva attacked the place along with their lord. The mountains tottered, the earth shook, the winds roared and the depths of the sea were disturbed. There is a description of the catastrophe in the Puranas; "Indra is knocked down and trampled on, Yama has his staff broken, Sarasvati and Matris have wounds on their nose, Bhaga has his eyes pulled out, Pushan has his teeth knocked down his throat, Chandra (the moon) is pummelled, Agni's hands are broken, Bhrigu's beard is crushed, Prajapatis are beaten and the gods are running helter and skelter". It was Vishnu who intervened and calmed the wrath of Shiva. Finally, Daksha acknowledged Shiva's supremacy and apportioned a due share to this god.

The second time Durga came to the world as Parvati, the daughter of Himalaya. As this was the rebirth of Sati, (the daughter of Daksha and the wife of Shiva,) in the second life too she wanted to become the consort of Shiva. But after the sacrifice of his first wife Shiva had lost all interest in marriage. Parvati now realised that practising penance was only one way of attracting his attention and winning his affection.

She undertook ascetic rites and recited prayer hymns for one thousand years to please god Shiva. Only then Shiva was convinced that Parvati was worthy of being accepted as his wife. The wedding of Shiva and Parvati is described in a very colourful manner in Puranic literature and a number of songs have been composed describing the marriage procession of Shiva which comprised of beggars, mendicants and wanderers.

As mentioned above goddess Durga has a variety of forms with different attributes. In her milder form she is Parvati (the mountain-girl), Uma (the light), Gauri (the yellow-complexioned beauty), Himavati (daughter of Himalaya), Jagatmata (mother of world) and Bhavani (the goddess of the universe); in her terrible form she is Durga (the inaccessible), Kali or Shyama (the black complexioned), Chandika or Chandi (the fearful one) and Bhairavi (the terrible). All these are broadly included under the name of Devi or Mahadevi (the great goddess).

The attainment of the name Durga, by Parvati is an interesting tale. On one occasion, sage Agastya asked Karttikeya why Parvati, his mother was called Durga. Karttikeya replied that some time back there was a demon, named Durg, the son of Ruru. He with his austerities pleased Brahma and by the god's blessings became very powerful. He conquered the three worlds and even dethroned Indra, the king of gods. Every one was afraid of him. He abolished all religious ceremonies as a result of which Brahmanas were terrified and stopped reading Vedas. All the gods assembled and prayed to god Shiva to protect them from the tyranny of this demon. Shiva took pity on them and asked Parvati to go and destroy the evil demon. She calmed the gods and accepted the commission. There ensued a long and fierce battle. As soon as the giant came near Parvati with his evil followers she assumed 1000 arms and also brought out a number of weapons out of her body. She repelled every attack and in the end the demon assumed the shape of a fearful buffalo and with his horns cast trees, rocks and mountains at the goddess, who in turn crushed everything into pieces. Then goddess Parvati pierced him with her trident and subdued him. The gods pleased with this deliverance praised the goddess and honoured Parvati with the name of Durga.

Another legend connected with Durga is that Mahishasura, a king of the demons, at a certain period overcame all the gods and reduced them all to the state of helplessness and incompetence. Indra together with all gods became very angry at the misdeeds of this demon and at the request of the suffering gods produced from their energy a goddess named Mahamaya or Durga. Streams of glory emanated from all gods and entered Mahamaya, who now resembled a mountain of fire and strength. This goddess killed the demon Mahishasura and delivered the gods from the distress.

The festival of Durga, celebrated during the month of Ashvin, is the most popular festival of Bengal. All the business in the state remains more or less suspended during the festival. The most important part of the festival is the making of the beautiful and costly images of the goddess. The image of Durga has ten arms. In one of her right hands is a long pointed spear, with which she is shown piercing the heart of demon Mahishasura, with one of her left hands she holds the hair of this giant. There are various other weapons in her other hands. Against her right leg leans a lion and near her left leg lies the demon subdued and defeated. Very frequently, small images of Lakshmi, Sarasvati, Karttikeya and Ganesha are also placed by the side of the goddess. At the close of the festival, these images are immersed into the river.

According to Markandeya Purana the goddess Durga has assumed ten different forms in order to destroy two great demons, Shumbha and Nishumbha. It is said that at the close of the Tretayuga, these two giants by their austerities had obtained great powers. Being exalted above the gods they tried to subdue the gods. They achieved many victories and gods were reduced to a deplorable state of helplessness. Now the gods solicited the help of Brahma and Vishnu, who directed them to Shiva. Shiva advised them to pray to Durga, who only can defeat the two demons. Finally when gods appealed to Durga for ending their troubles, she agreed.

Durga assumed the form of a beautiful woman and first enticed the minds of the two demons. Both of them enchanted by her beauty sent their best generals with a huge army to capture this female. These two generals named Chanda and Munda went to the Himalayas but were defeated and killed by the goddess and her mount, the divine lion. Now the two giants, Shumbha and Nishumbha, themselves marched to the Himalayas to capture Durga. These two demons had a general who had a blessing that the drops of blood falling on the ground from his body would create thousands of demons. Finally Durga was able to annihilate him, only when Durga's two forms namely Chandi and Kali both combined to neutralise this blessing. In the fierce engagement the goddess opened her mouth and drank every drop of blood before it fell on the ground while the other counterpart fought the demons and the general together. Eventually both the giants were killed.

Markandeya Purana places the ten forms of Durga in the following order. (1) Durga, the goddess who assumed a beautiful form to entice the demons;(2) Dashabhuja, in the form with which she destroyed a part of the army of demons; (3) Simhavahini, the one who fought with Raktavija, the general whose drops of blood created thousands of demons;(4) Mahisha-Mardini, who slew Shumbha, the demon, who had taken the form of a buffalo;(5) Jagaddhatri, one who overcame the army of demons; (6) Kali, the one who destroyed Raktavija by drinking the drops of blood and not allowing them to fall on the ground; (7) Muktakeshi, one with flowing hair who again overcame another army of the demons; (8) Tara who killed Shumbha; (9) Chinnamushtika, the one who killed Nishumbha; (10) Jagadgauri, who was worshipped by all the gods for their salvation. Some of these images of Durga are quite popular.

Simhavahini : In this form Durga is benign as well as belligerent. She is represented as the goddess with yellow garments and a glittering crown. She is shown sitting on a lion with either four, eight or ten hands. One hand is always shown bestowing a blessing on the worshippers. This image is very popular in the whole of north India and nightlong prayers (Jagaratras) are held in temples or in homes by devotees. Devotional songs are sung and in the early morning the worship comes to a close.

Tara : In this form the goddess is shown as a fierce black woman with four arms with one foot on the breast of Shiva, her consort. In one hand she holds a sword covered with blood; in another she has a demon's head while the remaining two are holding other lethal weapons. The foot on Lord Shiva's breast denotes the legendary tale of bloodthirsty Durga's anger against the demons which could not be controlled and as she continued destruction, Lord Shiva squatted on her path. When she put her foot on him, she immediately realised that she was treading upon her consort and her anger subsided.

Kali : This is the ferocious aspect of Durga perfectly personified. According to the Puranas, this image of Durga as Kali, so widely worshipped in eastern parts of India, owes its origin to the battle of Durga with Shumbha and Nishumbha. She after her victory over these demons was so overjoyed that she started the dance of death. Here the story resembles to that of Tara. In her great ecstasy Kali continued the destruction. As the prayers of all gods could not calm her, Lord Shiva had to intervene. Unable to dissuade her the god threw himself amongst the bodies of slain demons. When Durga saw that she was dancing over the body of her husband, she put her tongue out of her mouth in sorrow and surprise. She remained stunned in this posture and this is how Kali is shown in images with the red tongue protruding from her mouth.

Adhyatma Ramayana gives another story of the origin of Kali. It says that when Rama returned home with Sita after destroying Ravana, he boastfully narrated the stories of his victories to Sita. She smiled and said, "You rejoice because you have killed a Ravana with ten heads. But what shall you do with a Ravana with one thousands heads?" Rama very proudly boasted that he would destroy that demon too. Rama accepted his wife's challenge and collected his whole army and the army of all his allies and started for Shatadvipa, the abode of this new demon with one thousand heads. This new Ravana was a powerful demon. When attacked he discharged three magic arrows from his bow. One of these sent all the monkeys to Kishkindhya, their place of residence; another sent the army of Vibhishana, who was an ally of Rama and the ruler of Lanka after Ravana's death, back to their region beyond seashore; while the third arrow sent all soldiers of Rama back to Ayodhya, Rama's capital. Rama felt humiliated and then Sita laughingly assumed the form of terrific Kali; she attacked this new Ravana. After a long fight she killed the demon, drank his blood and began to dance and toss about the limbs of his body. It was Shiva who calmed her. However, this story has not received much popular approval.

In the images commonly worshipped Kali is shown as an extremly black female with four arms. In one hand she has a scymitar, in another the head of a demon, which she holds by his hair, the third hand is spread flatly open bestowing blessings and in the fourth she holds another weapon, usually a spear. She wears two heads of demons in place of earrings and has a necklace made of skulls. Her tongue is blood red and hangs down upon her chin. Blood is also seen streaming from her tongue and upon her body. She is shown standing with one foot on the breast of Shiva and the other rests on his thigh.

Animal sacrifice is done for Kali to please her and she is the favourite goddess of the dacoits, who believe that they will be saved from all dangers by the grace of Kali. At Kali Ghat, near Calcutta the most celebrated image of Kali is situated. Other forms of Kali are Chamunda, Shamshan Kali (goddess of the cremation ground), Bhadra Kali, Ugra Chandi, Bhima Chandi, Sidheshvari, and Sheetla (the goddess of smallpox). People also worship her to protect their children from dreaded diseases and their homes from ill omens.

Chamunda : As the name implies, in this form Durga, killed two demons, Chanda and Munda. From the forehead of Durga sprang a goddess of jet-black complexion, robed in the hide of an elephant, with a garland of dead corpses, with red-hot eyes and a long tongue. She gave out a loud shout and jumped upon the two demons. After this, episode goddess Durga is also known as Chamunda or Chamundi.

Durga, in fact, is the goddess most widely worshipped throughout India in various ways and in various names and forms.

KAMADHENU

Kamadhenu, the sacred cow, is a part and parcel of Hindu mythology. She is the cow, which grants all wishes and desires. She is the cow of plenty which emerged from Samudramanthana (the churning of the ocean) and was taken by the seven gods, who comprise the constellation of the Great Bear in the sky. She is also called Surabhi, Shaval, Aditi and Kamaduh. She is the mother of all cows.

According to mythological accounts, Brahma created the Brahmans and the cow at the same time-the Brahmans were to recite Vedas and scriptures while the cow was to afford ghee (clarified butter) for burnt-offerings in religious sacrifices. The cow is deemed to be the mother of gods and is declared by Brahma to be a proper object of worship. The unclean places are purified with cow-dung and in rural areas still the cow-dung is used to rub the ground of the doorway which is the first act in the morning.

Cow worship is performed by orthodox Hindus on the first of Vaishakha, when the cow was created by Brahma. The milkmen paint the horns and hoofs of their cattle yellow or saffron and bathe them in the river. 'The belief is, whoever kills a cow or allows another to kill it, shall rot in hell as many years as there are hairs upon this body'. A child born under unlucky stars is passed under the body of a cow to offset the evil effects.

Moreover cow plays a very important role in the cult of God Krishna. It follows the cowherd Krishna through his life on earth and also symbolises with its four legs the four Vedas of Hindus. Every part of cow's body has religious significance. Its horns symbolise the gods, its face the sun and the moon, its shoulders Agni, the god of fire, and its legs the Himalayas. Even Mahatma Gandhi was a great advocate of cow's protection and called it the 'gift of God'

Cow also symbolises Dharma. It is said to have stood steadily upon the earth with its four feet during the Satyuga (world's first age of truth), upon three feet during the Tretayuga (the second stage less perfect), upon two feet during the Dvaparayuga (the third stage of dwindling and disappearing perfection) and only on one leg during Kaliyuga (the fourth and current age of decadence).

GARUDA

Garuda with the head and wings of eagle and sometimes with the rest of his body like that of man, is called the king of birds and he is also the carrier of god Vishnu.

Garuda is the subject of numerous mythological stories in Mahabharata and other Puranas. Vinita, the wife of Kashyapa, the progenitor of gods and men, laid an egg and became the mother of this bird-god. As soon as Garuda was born, his body expanded and touched the sky, his eyes were like lightning; the mountains trembled as he spread his wings. It is stated that as a result of a dispute between Vinita, the mother of Garuda, and Kadru, the mother of serpents, a continuous enmity has been going on between the two and Garuda is on the look out to devour all the serpents he can find.

The story of his becoming the carrier of god Vishnu is related thus. Garuda with his great strength surmounted many dangers. At last one day Garuda seized the moon and concealed it under his wings. This worried all the gods in heaven and under the leadership of Indra the gods attacked Garuda. He overcame all gods but could not conquer Vishnu. However, when Garuda relented, god Vishnu made the bird immortal and granted him the honour of becoming His carrier.

Garuda is also said to have stolen Amrita (ambrosia) from the gods in order to purchase his mother's freedom from the thraldom of Kadru, the mother of a thousand powerful many-headed serpents. Indra discovered this theft and fought a fierce battle with Garuda. The amrita was recovered but the thunderbolt of Indra was smashed in the battle.

Garuda is identified with the all consuming sun's rays and popular belief credits him with the power to cure those who are victims of snakebite. There is a mantra (hymn) that is effective in such cases. "Om Tarakshya (Garuda), cast down my enemies, trample the diseases and venom that might invade me". The emerald stone traditionally deemed as the antidote of poison, is also associated with Garuda.

Garuda is also known by another name Vinayaka, which he shares with god Ganesha. Thus this god bird is thought to be the remover or destroyer of obstacles. Garuda is not worshipped widely as an independent god; he is worshipped together with Vishnu. His image is placed near Vishnu in temples and in pictures he is shown as carrying Vishnu in the skies on its back.

The elder brother of Garuda is called Uruda or Aruna and he is the charioteer of Surya, the sun god. The image of this bird is shown as that of a man without thighs.

The name of Garuda's son is Jatayu. This bird tried to rescue Sita, when Ravana was fleeing after kidnapping her. Ravana fights him and wounds him fatally. Rama himself cremated this bird and sent it to heaven.

SHESHANAGA

Sheshanaga (the serpent god) holds an important position in the Hindu mythology. As the reclining couch and the roofing canopy of the god Vishnu, it has been a god venerated by all and worshipped by many for centuries.

He is considered to be the king of the serpent race and the ruler of the infernal regions called patal. God Vishnu sleeps over the bed of its coil during intervals of creation. Sheshanaga is also represented as one supporting the world in its hood.

The Nagas have three kings, Vasuki, Takshaka and Shesha. Shesha is believed to represent the 'remainder' when the universe is destroyed and the power of creation (Lord Vishnu) rests on its coils.
The Nagas are dwelling in an underworld, called Nagaloka, which is an immense domain crowded with palaces, houses, towers and pleasure gardens. According to Varaha Purana, three of the lower worlds, Patal, Atala and Sutala belong to the Nagas. Their favourite places of visitations are the banks of river, Ikshumati; the Naimisha forest on the shores of the Gomati, the northern banks of the Ganga and the Nishada land. They also dwell under the sea.

These Nagas are not always the enemy of man and they even intermarry with them. Arjuna of Mahabharata married a Naga girl named Uloopi. Sheshanaga is the serpent with a thousand heads and is also called 'Ananta', the timeless, because it does not die with the destruction of the universe.

All serpents are of divine extraction, because they are the children of Kadru, who herself is the descendant of Kashyapa. The main city of Nagas is Bhogavati (the city of pleasures), where Shesha appears like a white mountain adorned with gems. The later Puranas identify Shesha even with Krishna and Vishnu. Shesha is considered to be the soul of Krishna's brother Balarama. Thus Shesha emerged from the body of dying Balarama and entered into the earth, where he was warmly welcomed by all other serpents.

AIRAVATA

Airavata, the white elephant and the king-god of elephants, is the mount of god Indra. This elephant emerged out from the ocean, during the process of Samudramanthan (churning of the ocean). That is why its name is derived from Iravat signifying one produced from water. Elephant is the mount of each one of the eight guardian deities who preside over the eight points of the compass.

The deities presiding over the four cardinal and four intermediate points of the compass are: (1) East-Indra; (2) Southeast-Agni; (3) South-Yama; (4) Southwest-Surya; (5) West-Varuna; (6) Northwest-Vayu;(7) North-Kuvera; (8) Northeast-Soma. Each of these deities has an elephant who takes part in the defence and protection of the allotted quarter. The chief among them is Airavata of Indra. He is also called Ardh-Matanga (elephant of the clouds), Arkasodara (brother of the sun), Nagamalla (the fighting elephant). The name of the wife of elephant Airavata is Abharamu.

Airavata has four tusks and is spotless white; he was made King of all elephants by Prithu, according to the Vishnu Purana. As per legends, Brahma held in his hands two halves of an eggshell over which he read seven sacred hymns. From the right half portion of the egg eight elephants including Airavata emerged and from the left half eight elephant calves. Another interesting myth is that initially all the elephants had wings, and they could fly in the skies. Once one of these flying elephant descended heavily on a tree under which a sage was performing his Puja (worship-rituals). The branches of the tree broke and sage felt much disturbed. He laid a curse upon all elephants that they should lose their wings. Notwithstanding this curse, they are still believed to be capable of producing clouds. Hence Indra, when seated on Airavata, sends rains on the earth.

The cult of the white elephants as sacred deities is widely practised in some other parts of Asia like Thailand and Burma.

BRIHASPATI

Brihas-pati or 'prayer-lord' is a name used alternatively in the Rig Veda with Brahmanaspati to designate the Lord of Prayer, the preceptor (Guru) and counsellor of the gods, and their high priest and chief sacrificer. He is considered to be the heavenly prototype of the earthly purohita or family priest and an authority in the magical power of spells, invocations and prayers. An early law code is named after Brihaspati. He is believed to be related to the thunder-god.

In certain myths he is identified with Agni, and associated with Soma in sacrificial soma rites. He is spoken of as the son of the rishi Angiras. He is regent of the planet Jupiter and his chariot is drawn by eight pale horses. An early nastika philosopher Brihaspati, who put forth the nihilistic sutras is also sometimes identified with this Brihaspati, the teacher of gods. But unlike the latter the philosopher Brihaspati condemned religion and the priests. He also decried the study of the Vedas and denounced their authors.

Legend relates that he had seduced Mamata, the pregnant wife of Utathya for which misdeed his own wife Tara (or Taraka) was abducted by Soma the moon, thus giving rise to the Taraka-maya war, in which Soma was aided by Ushanas, Rudra and the whole host of daityas (demons) and danavas (titans). Eventually Brahma intervened and restored Tara to her husband. After sometime, Tara gave birth to a son, Budha whom both Brihaspati and Soma claimed as theirs, until the child's mother settled the dispute by declaring that Soma was the father. Brihaspati's son through Mamata, wife of Utathya, was Bharadvaja.

Brihaspati's other names are : Animisha-acharya, (the Unblinking Teacher) Chakshas (Brightness), Ijya (Teacher), Jiva (the Living), Didivr (Shining) Dhishana (the Wise), Girpati (Lord of Speech).

BUDDHA

A god like figure considered to have lived during the period between 568-583 BC is the founder of Buddhism. He was the son of Suddhodana a kshattriya king of Mongolian stock and a member of the Gautama clan of the Sakya tribe. Hence Buddha is often called Sakyamuni, the sage of the Sakyas. Buddha's own name was Siddhartha and his mother was Queen Maya (or Mayadevi), a Lichchhavi princess.

Many different legends are related about his birth and life. Some scholars incline to the view that the whole account of his life is legendary and his teachings a mixture of several ancient systems.

Before the birth of Buddha his father heard an angelic annunciation and there are also stories of a Virgin Birth and of homage paid by trees and water to the divine infant. Before his birth his mother, Maya, dreamed that four kings raised her to the Himalayas where their four queens bathed and clothed her in heavenly robes. Buddha in the form of a white elephant with a silver lotus in his trunk circled three times around the queen's bed, smote her right side and entered her womb. The queen told her dream to the king, and the brahmin soothsayers of the court, notably Asita, interpreted it saying that the queen would bear a child who would be either a great king or a great Buddha (Wise One), a fact later confirmed when the infant was found to have all the thirty-two major marks of greatness on his body.

After ten months when it was time for the birth of Buddha Maya went to the home of her father in Devadaha for the confinement. On the way she gave birth to the child under the sal trees in the Lumbini gardens near the town of Kapilavastu, the capital of the Sakya kingdom in the south-eastern foothills of Nepal, one hundred miles north of Banaras. Mayadevi was at that time forty-five years old, and when the child was born the udumbara tree, which is said to blossom only when a Buddha is born, put forth wondrous blooms. There were also many other signs and portents.

Maya died when her child was one week old, and he was reared by her sister, Mahaprajapati (or Gotami) who was the second wife of Suddhodana. The boy received an excellent education, mastered the arts of warfare, and absorbed the philosphy of his time, although one record says that his relatives complained of his abnormal pursuit of pleasure. At the age of nineteen the prince married his cousin Yasodhara, daughter of Dandapani, and lived very happily with her.

Siddaratha's (was Buddha's original name) father, remembering the prophecy of Asita and fearing that his son might become an ascetic and leave the kingdom gave orders that all ugly things should be hidden from him. But Buddha's keen mind discerned the truth even behind apparent beauty.

One day he went out into the streets and saw an old man bent with age and he was struk with sorrow to think that all things if they live, must come to the stage of senility. On another occasion he saw a sick man and pondered on the problem of sickness and suffering. The sight of a corpse on yet another occasion led him to reflect on the end of life and the misery of existence. These sights were followed by a fourth, that of a tranquil ascetic with a begging bowl setting out to learn wisdom, and it marked the beginning of his conversion. It is said that while he sat reflecting on these four nimitta, 'signs', news was brought to him of the birth of his first (and only) child, a son, born after eight years of marriage. His reply to the news-bearer was 'Here is yet another bond to break'. He named his son Rahula, 'fetter'.

One night, six days after the birth of his son he awoke suddenly, greatly perturbed in spirit. He called Chauna (or Chhandaka) his charioteer and bade him saddle his horse Kanthaka. He then softly stole to his wife's chamber to look for the last time upon his wife and son. The child was asleep next to its mother whose hand was laid upon its head. He felt an overwhelming urge to take up his son in a farewell embrace, but the fear of waking his wife prevented him. Turning away he went out into the moonlight to Chauna waiting with the horse, and rode off into the night. He was at that time twenty-nine years of age. This incident is referred to as the Mahabhiniskkramana (maha abhi-nishkramana, 'great-over-leaving') or The Great Renunciation.

As he rode, Mara, the Prince of Evil, appeared to him and tempted him with the offer of great empires, but Buddha did not heed him. After crossing the small Anoma river he cut off his long black hair and sent it home with Chauna declaring that he would never return till 'he had conquered old age, disease and death'. He next exchanged his clothes with a ragged beggar and at last felt free to pursue his search for enlightenment.

He first went to Vaishali, put himself under a guru but feeling dissatisfied he went to Rajagriha and studied under another Guru.

He then repaired to Uruvela a village near Gaya, and here he was joined by five mendicant friars. For six years he devoted himself to the severest forms of penance and asceticism. He lived on seeds and herbs and for a time even on dung;gradually he came down to a single grain of rice a day. He let dust and dirt accumulate on him; he frequented burial and burning places and slept with rotting corpses. But enlightenment did not come and he felt that no wisdom could be attained by tapas or asceticism. He finally resolved to abandon this futile method, and when one day he fell unconscious through exhaustion and weakness, he was revived and offered a dainty meal in a golden dish by Sujata, daughter of a rich villager. Taking this as an omen he gave up asceticism, much to the displeasure of the five friars, who thereupon deserted him. He next went to a place called Bodhgaya (or Budhagaya), near the banks of the Nairanjana river; where he sat down to meditate under the shade-giving pipal (fig) tree, and here he resolved to stay until enlightenment came to him. This tree later became known as the Bo or Bodhi tree, because it was under its branches that, after seven weeks of meditation, he at last obtained the supreme knowledge he sought. At that historic site there now stands the Mahabodhi temple.

On the full moon day in the month of Vaisakha in the year variously dated between 533 and 528 BC as he sat wrapt in meditation he had a sudden vision of the endless succession of births and deaths. He saw that birth involved evil, and that rebirth was the inevitable lot of all mankind. Then like the light of dawn the solution to this perplexing problem came to him. He is said to have remained sitting in a state of profound trance for a full night and a full day, for he had attained Bodhi (Enlightenment) or Sambodhi (Full Enlightenment). He was thirty-five years old at the time. From then on he was honoured as the Buddha (Wise or Enlightened One) and later as Tathagata. Buddha now started preaching that continued for forty-five years.

He proceeded to Banaras and delivered his first sermon to his five original companions who at first listened with scepticism but were soon convinced. This famous first sermon, the Dharma-chakra-pravartana, or Setting in Motion the Wheel of the Law, was delivered in the Deer Park (Mrigadava) at Sarnath near Banaras. His band of disciples soon increased as he went from town to town preaching the new doctrine. At Uruvela he delivered the famous Fire Sermon to a group of fire-worshippers, and converted them.

Buddha's discourses were not in Sanskrit but in the language easily understood by people. It had the form of Socratic questioning, parables, formulas and sutras (sermons). At the end of one of his sermons the whole world shook; a tree sprouted up from his toothpick; he subdued fierce animals with love; he visited the Tavatimsa heaven where he was welcomed by Indra and preached to the devas, and many others of similar import.

Buddha's fame spread all over India, and thousands of people including householders, merchants, peasants and princes became his disciples and followers. A monastry was built in the Jetavana grove, presented by a wealthy convert, which became the headquarters of Buddha's ministry. Buddha travelled far and wide. He came to Kapilavastu and visited his home, parents, his wife and son. His son, Rahula also joined the Buddhist order along with some other relatives.

Some of his famous followers were Ananda his cousin, the 'blessed intimate' of Buddha and his chief disciple; Kassapa (Kashyapa) the most learned of his disciples; the rich youth Yasa; the king Bimbisara and the barber Upali.

A lifelong enemy of Buddha was his another cousin, Devadatta. His rivalry towards Buddha started when both were very young. This continued even when Buddha's fame had spread far and wide. Devadatta made three attempts on his life. He had employed assasins to kill Buddha but they were converted by Buddha. The second attempt by throwing a rock at him also failed. In his third attempt he let loose a wild elephant against Buddha, but the animal listened docilely to his sermon and went back without harming him. Towards the end of the life Devadatta also embraced Buddhism.

Buddha founded the Sangha or Buddhist order of monks whose following grew rapidly. The monks were not allowed to have any personal property; they were to beg for their food, wear coarse clothes, and live a simple life. The order consisted of sravaka (hearers or laymen), upasaka (lay disciples), bhikku (bhikshu, or religious mendicants), and sramana (ascetics). An order of bhikkuni or nuns was also started at the repeated entreaty of his disciples as Buddha was reluctant to do so, and among the first members to join was his wife Yasodhara.

Traditional stories hold that Buddha died under a sal tree at Kusinara (or Kusinagara) the district now known by the name Gorakhpur, at the age of eighty. This is referred to as his Pari-nirvana, 'final extinction'. His last words were, 'Subject to decay are all component things. Strive earnestly to work out your own salvation'.

Seven days after his death his remains were cremated. The ashes were divided into ten parts and given to the rajas of the land where Buddha had lived, worked and died. Stupas and dagobas (reliquary chambers) were erected over the places where they were buried.

Buddha was strongly opposed to religious ritual, to ceremonial worship and the sacrificial system, and condemned the whole idea of the caste system as false. He laid much stress on self-sufficiency. He taught that the soul does not exist and said that the soul is in reality a physical and mental aggregate of five impermanent conditions—the physical body, feelings, idea or understanding, will and pure consciousness.

DAKSHA

Daksha which means 'dexterous', is a primordial creative rishi of uncertian provenance who in different texts is referred to as a Prajapati, a Visvadeva, an Aditya and a Manu.

Daksha is variously described as a son of Brahma springing from the right thumb of the god; as emerging from the all-encompassing Aditi and himself creating Aditi; as the father and offspring of the moon; and, in a second incarnation, as the son of the rishi Prachetas by Marisha; or as an incarnation of Vishnu.

One myth has it that Daksha, the first of all males, himself took on the form of a beautiful woman, by whom he had many daughters. Another states that he married Prasuti (daughter of Priyavrata and granddaughter of Svayambhuva Manu) by whom he had, according to different accounts, twenty-five, fifty or sixty daughters. In his second incarnation he had seven sons.

Daksha's many daughters play a prominent part in Hindu mythology. One of them, Sati, married Shiva and in consequence of a quarrel between her husband and her father, she committed suicide. A later legend relates that Brahma once invited the gods and great rishis to a feast. Daksha arrived late and all the gods rose respectfully to greet him, except Shiva. Daksha angered at the insult left the hall planning vengeance. He arranged a great sacrifice (for Vishnu, according to the Puranas), to which he invited all the gods except Shiva. The sage Dadhicha informed Shiva and his wife Sati about this, and the latter mortified beyond endurance at her own father's treatment of her husband threw herself into the flames of the sacrificial fire.

At this Shiva got infuriated and determined to stop the sacrificial festivities. For this purpose he created a dreadful being from his mouth, the thousand-headed, thousand-armed Virabhadra, who held the dread weapons of destruction, the discus, the mace, the bow, the battle-axe and the trident. This monster caused consternation among the assembled guests, while Shiva wreaked his vengeance amongst them.

The rishis tried to appease Shiva but in vain. He decapitated the insolent Daksha with his blazing trident. The gods and rishis humbly propitiated the offended deity, apportioned to him the choicest share of the sacrifice, and restored the damage he had done. Daksha's severed head could not be found so it was replaced by that of a goat or ram.

DHANVANTARI

Dhanvan-tari, which means 'arrow-moving', is a deity of probably aboriginal Indian antiquity. His name suggests the parabolic flight of an arrow and he was early identified with the sun, since the sun also 'moved in an arc'. In popular mythology he was the son of the sage Dirghatamas and physician of the gods, who appeared during the Churning of the Ocean carrying the vessel containing medicines. According to tradition, Ayurveda or the science of health and medicine is attributed to him.

Certain myths consider him to be a part of Vishnu himself, whereas others consider him as a disciple of Shiva, and still others consider him as a pupil of the eagle-god Garuda, and the conqueror of the malignant power of the serpent people. The name Dhanvantari was also borne by a legendary teacher of medicine and author of numerous treatises on Ayurveda, and by one of the 'nine gems' at the court of King Vikramaditya.

KAMADEVA

Kama, or the god of love, has to his credit many legendary stories regarding his origin. In the Vedas, Desire is said to have been the first thing that stirred in the Deep at the dawn of creation, and in the Atharva Veda Kama is exalted as a creator. He is sometimes identified with Agni, god of fire, or with a superior form of Agni. Certain myths consider him to be the son of Dharma, god of justice and Sraddha, goddess of faith; or the son of Lakshmi, goddess of wealth; or the son of Brahma; or as having been born of the waters. Kama's wife, Rati (sexual desire) was a daughter of Daksha. She is portrayed holding a small mirror (darpana) in her hand since she arouses wantonness.

According to one legend Kama was directed to arouse love-thoughts in Shiva who was so abosorbed in meditation that the demon Taraka assumed control over the universe. Kama succeeded in his mission but incurred the anger of Shiva who reduced him to ashes with a flash from his third eye. Later on Kama was allowed to survive as Ananga, 'bodiless', and live in the minds of all beings. Another legend says that Shiva finally relented and allowed Kama to be reborn as Pradyumna son of Krishna and Rukmini.

Kama is also considered to be the lord of the apsaras and is depicted as a handsome youth riding on a cuckoo or a parrot, attended by the celestial nymphs. The god is armed with a bow made of sugar-cane, with a bow-string of bees, and carries a quiver of arrows each tipped with a flower. There is a festival attributed to Kama called Madanotsava, described by Kalidasa, Sriharsha and others. A festival marked by general feasting and unrestrained merry making like dancing, singing and games, in which kings and beggars, brahmins and lower castes took part with equal enthusiasm, and which was climaxed by the promiscuous love chase and union.

Kama is also called: Atma-bhu (self-existent); Abhi-rupa, (beautiful); Darpaka (wanton); Gridhu (eager); Ira-ja (water-born); Ishma (inciting); Kala-keli (diverting); Kama-deva, (love-god); Kandarpa (satisfier); Kanjana (appeaser); Kinkira (enslaving); Karshni (son of Krishna); Kharu (desirous); Kantu (happy); Kusum-ayudha (flower-armed); Mada (wanton); Madana (drunk with love); Mara (destroyer); Makara-ketu (crocodile-banner); Manmatha (agitator); Mano-ja (mind-produced); Madhu-dipa (honey-lamp); Muhura (bewildered); Murmura (crackling like a fire); Pushpa-bana (flower-arrow); Pushpa-dhanus (flower-bow); Pushpa-sara (flower-dart); Pancha-sayaka (five-arrows); Ramana (dalliance); Raga-vrinta (passion-stalk); Rupastra (beauty-weapon); Rata-naricha (lover of women); Sri-nandana (gladdener); Samantaka (ender of peace); Samara (rememberer); Titha (fire); Vama (handsome).

KUVERA

Kuvera or Kubera which means, 'ugly-body' is a late Vedic lord of evil spirits whose abode was in the shades. He was the son of either Pulastya or Visravas, and appears in the Ramayana as Vaisravana, half-brother of the ten-headed Ravana. His first residence, Lanka, situated on Mount Meru was according to the Bhagavata Purana, a city of vast extent and unequalled magnificence built of gold by Visvakarman the celestial architect. Ravana drove Kuvera from Lanka but Vayu the wind god broke off the summit of Mount Meru with Lanka and hurled it into the sea where it came to rest as an island, now called Ceylon. Here Ravana took possession of the city and became the most famous of the kings of Lanka.

In Ravana's time it was described as surrounded by seven concentric moats, deep and broad, filled with pure water, in which fierce aquatic animals lived. Four bridges spanned the outer moat around the first circumambient wall which was pierced by four massive gates. On the walls there were mechanical contivances to ward off invaders by means of fire, water and stones. A series of seven such concentric walls, each build of a different metal and each garrisoned by armed warriors, surrounded the fabled city of Lanka. After Kuvera has been dispossessed he moved his realm to Alaka in the celestial enclosure of paradise.

Kuvera performed penances for a thousand years until Brahma promised that he would be given immortality and be made one of the guardian deities of the world. Brahma gave him the self-moving aerial car called Pushpaka which was described as ratna-varshuka (jewel-raining) since it contained within it a magnificent bejewelled pavilion which glistened brilliantly as it moved through the air. It was taken away from Kuvera by Ravana but was finally restored to Kuvera.

Kuvera is regent of the north, and the lord of all the gold, silver, gems and other treasures of the earth. Chief among them are the nine mystic 'nidhi' or treasures (also spoken of as nidhana or hidden; nikara or abundant; sevadhi or hoarded) which are named as follows : (1) kachchhapa (tortoise); (2) kunda or mukunda (jasmine); (3) nanda (delight); (4) kharva, (innumerable); (5) makara (crocodile); (6) nila (sapphire); (7) shanka (conch); (8) padma-raga (ruby); and (9) mahapadma, (great lotus). Each nidhi has its own guardian spirit and is an object of worship by Tantriks.

Kuvera is served by the yaksha (or yakshi) a class of elemental beings referred to as punya-jana, (propitious folk), mostly benevolent though sometimes evil, whose chief is Manibhadra. They are the custodians of treasures hidden in the roots of trees and are thus often called sylvan or earth spirits. The most valiant of the yakshas watch over the mighty riches hidden in the Himalayas. Some yakshas are of the size of men, some are giants, some are dwarfs.

A a class of 'hidden beings' known as Guhyaka, led by Revanta son of Surya, serves Kuvera by helping him guard the hidden treasure. The horse-headed, bird-bodied kimnara (what-men?) or kinnara, also part of Kuvera's entourage, are sometimes called the sons of the Rishi Kashyapa and are said to have sprung from the toe of Brahma. Like the gandharvas they were the celestial choristers and musicians of Kuvera's realm. Associated with the kimnaras and later identified with them are the kimpurusha (kim-purusha, 'what-men?'), elf-like beings of a low order, partaking of the nature and appearance of both man and beast. They generally lived in the remoter ranges of the Himalayas and were ruled over by their own chiefs.

Kuvera had two wives, namely, Riddhi, 'prosperity', and Yakshi daughter of the danava (giant) Muru, and queen of the yakshis. His daughter was Minakshi, and his sons Manigriva (also called Varnakavi), and Nalakubara; the latter married the beautiful nymph Rambha who emerged during the Churning of the Ocean.

Kuvera is represented as a white man with eight teeth, three legs and a misshapen body covered with ornaments, and is often shown riding on a man. Among his names are: Vaisravana (from Vishravas); Paulastya (from Pulastya); Aidavida (from Idavida); Isa-sakhi (Shiva's friend); Ku-tanu (ill-bodied); Dhanada (wealth-giver); Dhanapati (wealth-lord); Ichchha-vasu, (ordaining wealth); Yaksha-raja (king of the yakshas); Mayu-raja (ruler of the Mayus); Rakshasendra (chief of the rakshasas); Ratna-garbha (jewel-bellied); Raja-raja (king of kings); Nara-raja (king of men).

MAHAVIRA

Mahavira is a godly figure believed to have lived during the period between 599-467 BC. He is considered to be the twenty-fourth tirthankara of the Jains, and the Jina of the present age. He was born as the, the second son of a nobleman of Vaishali, the capital of Videha (modern Bihar) and his name was Vardhamana. His father Siddharatha, was a prince of the Jnatrika clan, was a follower of Parsva, the twenty-third tirthankara. His mother Trisala was the sister of the governor of Vaishali and related to the ruling Lichchhavi house of Videha. Legend relates that during her pregnancy she had dreams portending the birth of a hero. The boy Vardhamana was therefore trained to be a warrior and in due time married Yashoda, a lady of noble birth, by whom he had one daughter, Anojja.

In his thirtieth year his parents left the mortal world, in accordance with to the teachings of their sect, by voluntary starvation. His elder brother Nandivardhana succeeded to the principality, while Vardhamana renounced the world and became an ascetic. He was borne from home in a palanquin to the shade of an Ashoka tree where he divested himself of his ornaments and fine raiment, and plucked out his hair. From then on, for thirteen years, till the age of forty-three, he led a life of extreme self-mortification. He discarded all clothing because he considered nudity essential to true asceticism and allowed vermin to infest his body since killing was contrary to the precepts of his faith.

At the end of this period while he was in the sunny field of a householder named Samaga near an old Hindu temple, under a sala tree on the banks of the river Rijupalika, squatting in deep meditation, with heels joined, knees high, and head low between them, he achieved the state called nirvana (cessation) or kaivalya (isolation). He was acclaimed as a tirthankara (ford-finder), kaivalin (supreme omniscient), jina (conqueror), and arhat (Blessed One), and one of the great spiritual teachers who are ordained to appear at regular intervals to enlighten mankind. He was thenceforth known as Mahavira, 'Great Hero'.

During his early life, while at Nalanda, he came into contact with Goshala, founder of the Ajivikas. The two ascetics lived together for six years, when, following a bitter quarrel, they separated. In a final encounter Goshala cursed Mahavira, but the curse boomeranged upon Goshala and he himself died. A few days later Mahavira was taken ill, as a consequence of the curse, but made a quick recovery, 'after eating the flesh of a cockerel killed by a cat'. Mahavira had eleven disciples known as ganadhara (multitude-grippers).

Unlike Buddha, Mahavira did not preach to the masses, but his teachings had a great effect upon kings and intellectuals, and spread mostly to the west and south of India. To the four vows of Parsva he added a fifth, that of aparigraha (non-ownership) and is said to have introduced the practice of confession into Jainism. Mahavira founded a celibate clergy and an order of nuns. He died at the age of seventy-two, at Pavapuri in the Patna district.

PARSURAM

The youngest son of the sage Jamadagni and his beautiful wife Renuka, is regarded as the sixth avatara or 'descent' of Vishnu to earth. But interestingly, Parsuram was a worshipper of Shiva and enjoyed the protection of Shiva. It was God Shiva who instructed him in the use of arms and gave him the parasu, a magic battle-axe, in honour of which he was called Parsuram, 'Rama of the Axe'. In the Ramayana he makes a brief appearance, in an encounter with Rama. He became angry with Rama for having broken the bow of Shiva in the contest for Sita's hand and he challenged him to a fight, but was defeated and also 'expelled from a seat in the celestial world'. In the Mahabharata he teaches both Karna and Arjuna the use of arms, and has a duel with Bhima in which both heroes suffer equally. Subsequently he takes part in the war council of the Kauravas. Mahabharata relates another incident where, in obedience to his father's order, he strikes off his mother's head with his axe. But later on at Parsuram's request, Jamadagni restores her to life.

The Haihaya king Kartavirya was Parsuram's great enemy. This kshattriya monarch once visited the hermitage of Jamadagni when the sage and his sons were out, and was welcomed by the sage's wife with due hospitality. Unmindful of the respect and hospitality shown to him the warrior king destroyed the trees around the hermitage and then tried to lay hands on the sacred cow belonging to Jamadagni, the calf of Kamadhenu, which the hermit had acquired through penance. The calf miraculously conjured up a troop of Yavanas who repulsed Kartavirya, but he returned again and bore the calf away. When Parsuram heard this on his return he became very angry, pursued the plundering king, cut off his thousand arms and slaughtered him like a common animal. On the advice of his father, Parsuram then set out on a pilgrimage to atone for the sin of killing Kartavirya. While Parsuram was on pilgrimage the sons of Kartvirya went to the hermitage of Jamadagni, and in retaliation to the killing of their father slew the sage in cold blood as he sat deep in meditation.

Parsuram's ire now knew no bounds. While his father's body was being cremated he took a solemn vow before the gods that he would exterminate the whole race of the accursed kshattriyas. He first massacred the sons of Kartavirya, and then embarked upon his famous expeditions. It is believed that he cleared the earth of the kshattriya clans twenty one times filling with their blood the great lakes of Samanta-panchaka and Kurukshetra.

Parusuram begged Varuna, god of the sea, to give him land that he might bestow it upon the brahmins in expiation for the sin commited by him by slaughtering the kshattriyas, whereupon Varuna, withdrew the ocean from the hills of Gokarna as far as Cape Comorin and presented him with the country of Malabar. In some legends it is said that Parsuram himself drove back the ocean and so increased the territory, and cut fissures in the Ghats with blows of his axe. He then settled down in this area, known as Aparanta, 'west-end', with brahmins from the north, and bestowed the whole territory on the maharishi Kashyapa. The entire west coast of India, from Bhrigukachchha down to Cape Comorin still retains its association with Parsuram.

The hero finally retired to the Mahendra mountains (the Eastern Ghats), where he was visited by gods and heroes, including Arjuna. He is said to be chiranjiva or immortal, and is believed to be still alive in some cave in Central India. Parsuram's wife was Dharani, 'earth', an incarnation of Lakshmi the eternal spouse of Vishnu.

SATI

Sati meaning 'true' is, a daughter of the sage Daksha. When she came of age her father arranged a svayamvara so that she might choose her husband, and invited all the gods except Shiva whom Daksha hated. Sati however loved Shiva and at the svayamvara she went around the hall with the garland in her hand thinking devotedly of her Shiva. While thus lost in contemplation she threw the garland into the air mentally offering it to the god. And at that instance Shiva manifested himself and the garland fell around his neck, and Daksha was obliged to accept him as his son-in-law.

The enmity between the two continued even after this. Once when Daksha entered the hall where his son-in-law was seated with other deities, Shiva did not rise to greet him as the other gods did. Later when Daksha gave a sacrificial feast he did not invite Shiva, which resulted in a disaster. Daksha's failure to invite her husband so mortified Sati that she created the sacrificial fire known as Jvala-mukhi, 'fire-mouth', into which she threw herself and was consumed. The site is now said to be a small extinct volcano in the lower Himalayas north of the Punjab, and is a place of pilgrimage. After this incident the term sati was applied to all widows and wives who immolated themselves.

According to one legend Sati was changed into a kokila (cuckoo); in another version she was reborn as the goddess Uma. In yet another,

Shiva restored her to life by picking up her charred body and dancing round the world with it seven times. But the popularly accepted story goes that Shiva recovered her corpse from the sacrificial fire and carried it on his head as a penance. Vishnu feared that Shiva might obtain excessive power by this means and so with successive throws of his discus cut the body into bits. It scattered on earth in a number of pieces (5, 51, 52, 72 or 108 pieces—the number varies in different versions), and each spot where it fell became a pitha (or pitha-sthana, 'seat-place'), a sacred centre of pilgrimage. There is a great deal of confusion about these places, as also about which particular part of Sati's body fell where. More than a thousand places in India claim the honour of having received one or more of the pieces, most of them claiming the ears, breasts, and organ of generation.

There are certain usually recognized pithas. Arbuda (Mount Abu) where the right breast of the goddess fell; its sanctity has been somewhat eclipsed by the numerous Jain shrines built in the area. Arasana (or Arasur) near Mount Abu; here the left breast of Sati-fell and here she is worshipped in the form of the goddess Ambika. Banaras where either the ear-rings or the left hand fell; the ear-rings give the name to the Manikarni pool at Banaras. Devipatan, 'goddess-fall', where the right hand descended. The ancient temple was despoiled by one of Aurangzeb's officers to whom a dire punishment was meted out. Faljur, in the Jaintia Parganas fell the left leg or the left knee-cap. Hinglaj in west Baluchistan, the forehead or the crown of the head of the goddess fell. Hinglaj is sometimes identified with a place on the river Sarasvati, not far from Siddhapur, in northern Gujarat. Jalandhara in the Panjab, where the right breast or nipple, or stomach descended. At Janashthana in the Deccan, the cheeks, and three hairs from the pubes fell. Jvalamukhi (or Jvalapur) in east Panjab, about four miles from Hardwar, the tongue, palate, scalp, foot or eye fell. Kalighat (near Calcutta) also known as Ukule Ghat, the fingers or great toe of the right foot of the goddess fell. Kamakhya, the place where the organs of generation descended. This place is regarded as one of the most important of the Sati pithas. In Kashmir (various places here claim the honour), the neck, ear, toe or knee descended. Labhpur, the place where the lips, chin, palate, teeth, pubes fell. In Madura the left eye or left breast, the left hand or rear portion fell. The temple of Minakshi stands on the site. Manasarovara at the foot of Mount Kailasa where the right palm of the goddess fell. Muktinath in Nepal, near the Gandaki river, the sex organs of Sati are said to have fallen. Patna (ancient Pataliputra) where the pat or garment covering the genitals fell. Purnagiri in Assam (some say near Poona), the buttocks, breasts or sex organs descended. Sugandha in southern Bengal, the nose, hair, right hand, the anus fell. Uddiyan identified with various places; the buttocks, the sex organs descended. In Ujjain, fell the elbow, now the site of the Harsiddhi temple. In Vindhyachal about five miles from Mirzapur in Uttar Pradesh the temple of Vindhya-vasani (or Kausiki) a form of the goddess Shakti is situated. It was once a famous abode of the thugs. It is believed that the toe of the left foot of Sati fell here.

VARUNA

A deity of Indo-European origin and the personification of the all-enveloping heaven. At first Varuna was the sustainer of the universe, the presiding deity of rita, or the moral order of the cosmos and the rightness underlying all things. In general his character far surpassed that of any other Vedic deity. Nothing was hidden from him; his pasa, (noose), caught the wicked; as a judge he rewarded righteousness and punished iniquity, but was ever forgiving to those who were penitent. It was believed that he made the sun shine in the heavens, the winds that blew was his breath, he was the one who hollowed out the channels of the rivers which flow at his command and that he made the depths of the sea.

But later, in the new environment of India there was a need scarcely less important than the regulation of metaphysical law, and that was the need for seasonal rain. Therefore Varuna's powers decreased and he was finally dethroned by Indra. He became the 'prince of oceans', commanding innumerable white horses, and as the Indian Neptune he received the worship of fishermen.

According to legends he once ran off with Bhadra wife of Utathya, but later he restored her. He is paid little homage in India today, and the only existing temple dedicated to him is on the island of Bali. Varuna's paradise is Vasudha-nagara (wealth-yielding town); his palace is Sukha (pleasant), situated on Pushpa-giri (flower-mountain). Over his throne, protecting him from the waters is the hood of the great serpent Abhoga. Varuna is regent of the west and his vahana or vehicle is the makara, or sea-monster.

Varuna was regarded as the chief of the Adityas, and as such was associated with the god Mitra who was his constant companion. But whereas Varuna represented the night heavens, Mitra was a god of daylight and of the sun. Mitra appears with Varuna in the mishap with the nymph Urvashi that resulted in the birth of the sages Vasishtha and Agastya.

Varuna is also called Prachetas (intelligent); Ambu-raja (water-king); Jala-pati (water-lord); Ad-dama (surrounder); Pasin or Pasa-bhrit (noose-carrier); Vari-loma (moist-haired); Yadah-pati (king of aquatic creatures); Yado-natha (lord of sea monsters). Makara, the vahana of Varuna, is also called Kantaka (thorny); Asita-danta (black-toothed); Jala-rupa (water-formed).

VAYU

Vayu holds a prominent place in the Vedas and is believed to have sprung forth from the breath of Purusha, and his chariot, pulled by a thousand horses, is driven by Indra, who acts as his charioteer. In later times his importance diminished, and he became a regent of the north-west quarter.

In the puranas and epics he is the king of the heavenly singers and the gandharvas, and the father of the Pandava prince, Bhima, and of the monkey chief Hanuman. Legend says it that once Vayu was invited by the sage Narada to break the summit of Mount Meru. The wind-god blew for a year with all his terrible might, but failed in his efforts because the eagle Garuda shielded the mountain with his wings. One day when Garuda was absent, he attacked the mountain and broke off the summit, hurling it into the sea, where it became the island of Lanka (Ceylon).

Certain legends consider Vayu to be a licentious and cruel god. Vayu is said to have made the hundred daughters of king Kusanabha hump-backed, because they did not submit to his embraces. This gave the name Kanya-kubja, 'maidens-crooked', to the king's capital city of Kanauj. Vayu is often used to symbolize strength, persistence, ruthlessness, omni-presence and other qualities.

Vayu is also called Vata; Pavana (god of physical strength); Anila (with whom are associated the forty-nine godlings of the wind); Gandha-vaha (perfume-bearer); Jala-kantara (whose forest is water); Sada-gati or Satata-ga (ever-moving).

In Vaiseshika, Vayu is described as one of the subtle elements; in Ayurveda it is one of the three bodily humours; in Yoga and Hindu philosophy it is the term of the vital energies or airs of the body. The term prana is generally used for the vital airs, and is also employed as a synonym for wind, breath, life, life-force and soul. The control of this vital breath through the practice of pranayama is one of the fundamental techniques of yoga. Traditionally ten vayus or vital airs are listed, divided into two groups of five each.

Pranadi are the winds of the inner body. They include the prana, apana, samana, udana and vyana. The prana, is a term universally adopted for all the vital airs, but specifically applied to the wind that has its seat in the heart. It is also called asu 'breath'. It is blood-red or yellow in colour and controls respiration. It is a forward wind, related to the east, and linked with the sun. The apana has its seat in the rectum, is purple and orange in colour, and controls ejection i.e. excretion and ejaculation. It is a down wind, of the west, linked with fire. Samana, has its seat in the navel, is white or green in colour, and controls digestion. It is a consummating wind, of the north, and of the clouds. Udana, has its seat in the throat, is pale blue, and controls speech and coughing. It is an upward wind, of the zenith, and of the sky. Vyana, moves all over the body, or has its seat in the genitals; is flame-coloured and controls the circulation. It is considered to be a reciprocal wind, of the south, and of the moon.

Nagadi are the five vayu belonging to the outer body. They are naga, kurma, krikara, devadatta and dhananjaya. Naga or 'snake' controls belching and clearing the throat. Kurma (tortoise), controls blinking, and the dropping of the eyelids in sleep. Krikara (partridge), controls sneezing, hunger and thirst. Devadatta (god-given), controls yawning and dozing. Finally dhanan-jaya (treasure-winning), controls hiccuping. It is also the air that remains in the body during coma, swoon or trance, and after death.

SWASTIKA

Swastika or Svastika is an auspicious symbol, an elaboration of the equal armed cross, but with the arms bent, hence also called the 'limbed cross'. Its name is said to be a combination of su (well) asti (is) ka (a noun ending) i.e., 'It is well'. The interjection svasti is used before and after pronouncing the sacred syllable Om, and during sacrificial ceremonies.

In Hinduism the swastika is believed to be derived either from the wheel, symbolically reduced to four spokes and set at right angles to indicate the cardinal points, or from the two firesticks of the Vedic sacrificial fire which were always set down in the form of a cross. As a fire and sun symbol it was also called the fire cross or solar cross.

This symbol was well known among the ancients. The archaeological discoveries in Egypt; in Hissarlik, site of Homer's Troy; in China, Greece, Scandinavia, Scythia, Mexico and Peru have proved its widespread usage. The swastika symbol is supposed to be marked on the hood of the cobra, and is often associated with the heliolithic culture of snake-worshipping peoples such as the Nagas.

In India two kinds of swastika are distinguished. The right hand or male, representing the vernal sun, where the right end of the horizontal bar has an arm bending downwards, with the ends of the other three arms moving in the same direction, so that the cross moves clockwise. It is so called because if one goes around the figure with one's right side towards the centre of the cross, one will move in the direction indicated by the bent arms. The left hand or female cross, representing the autumnal sun, goes in the opposite, anti-clockwise direction, and is considered inauspicious.

The auspicious swastika, a symbol of good luck, is often found stamped on various objects. A series of small swastikas are a very popular motif for border designs on textiles. The rainy season is especially devoted to its honour in Maharashtra, when women draw swastikas on floors and worship them.

A 'good luck' asana (yogic sitting posture) named swastikasana is sometimes assumed in meditation in the form of an 'inclosed' as distinct from an outstretched cross. Here two crosses are formed by squatting with crossed legs and with arms crossed over the breast.

DIAMOND POCKET BOOKS

SELECTED BOOKS FOR ALL

HEALTH SERIES

Title	Author	Price
Natural Healing with Reiki	Sukhdeepak Malvai	100.00
Unveiling the Secrets of Reiki	M. Subramaniam	195.00
Wonders of Magnetotherapy	Dr. S. K. Sharma	60.00
Nature Cure for Health & Happiness	Dr. Satish Goel	60.00
Family Homeopathic Guide	Dr. S. K. Sharma	75.00
Miracles of Urine Therapy	Dr. S. K. Sharma	40.00
Health in Your Hands	Dr. S. K. Sharma	80.00
Food for Good Health	Dr. S. K. Sharma	60.00
Juice Therapy	Dr. S. K. Sharma	60.00
Be Young & Healthy for 100 Year	Dr. Pushpa Khurana	50.00
Pregnancy & Child Care	Dr. Satish Goel	60.00
Causes & Cure of Blood Pressure	Dr. Satish Goel	60.00
Causes & Cure of Diabetes	Dr. Satish Goel	60.00
Ladies Slimming Course	Dr. Satish Goel	60.00
Be Your Own Doctor	Dr. Kanta Gupta	50.00
Acupuncture & Acupressure Guide	Dr. Satish Goel	80.00
The Awesome Challenge of AIDS	Dr. Pushpa Khurana	40.00
Yoga For Better Health	Acharya Bhagwan Dev	40.00
Ladies Health Guide (With Make-Up Guide)	Usha Rai Verma	75.00
Skin Care	Dr. Renu Gupta	60.00
Brilliant Light (Reiki Grand Master Manual)	M. Subramaniam	195.00
Ayurvedic Cure For Common Diseases	Acharya Vipul Rao	75.00
Low Calories Diet	Tehlina Kaul	95.00
Common Diseases of Women	Dr. Renu Gupta	75.00
Diseases of Respiratory Tract (Nose, Throat, Chest & Lungs)	Dr. Nistha	60.00
How to keep Fit	M. Kumaria	20.00
Causes & Cure of Heart Ailments	Dr. Satish Goel	60.00
Surya Chikitsa	Acharya Satyanand	60.00
Causes and Cure of Stress (Migraine & Headache)	Dr. Shiv Kumar	75.00
Acupressure Guide	Dr. Satish Goel	40.00
Acupuncture Guide	Dr. Satish Goel	40.00
Joys of Parenthood	Dr. R. N. Gupta	40.00
Sex for all	Dr. Satish Goel	50.00
Vatsyanana Kamasutra	Dr. B. R. Kishore	60.00
Manual of Sex & Tantra	Dr. B. R. Kishore	40.00
Tips on Sex	Dr. S. K. Sharma	75.00
Herbs That Heal	Acharya Vipul Rao	75.00
Causes, Cure and Prevention of Nervous Diseases	Dr. Shiv Kumar	75.00

LANGUAGES BOOKS

Title	Author	Price
Bengali Learning & Speaking Course	Amitabh Dhingra	25.00
Assamese Learning & Speaking Course	Debajit Saikia	30.00
Learning English through Assamese in 30 Days		25.00
Puzzle Pack	Ivar Utial	20.00
Book of Idioms & Pharases	P. Charles	20.00
Everyday Letters	Dr. B. R. Kishore	30.00
Hindi English Teacher	Dr. B. R. Kishore	20.00
Diamond Easy Bengali Conversation	Sameer Dey	25.00
Diamond Bengali Speaking Course	Sameer Dey	25.00
Learn Bengali through English		25.00
Learn English through Nepali	Dr. B. R. Kishore	20.00
Learn Urdu in 30 days through English	Prakash Nagaich	20.00
Learn English through Urdu in 30 days	Amitabh Dhingra	20.00
Learn Urdu through Hindi in 30 days		20.00
Learn Gujrati through English in 30 days		20.00
Letter Drafting Course	Veena Khanna	60.00

Diamond Pocket Books (P) Ltd. X-30, Okhla Industrial Area, Phase-II, New Delhi-110020

Our Books at a Glance

SELECTED BOOKS ON RELIGION & SPIRITUALITY

RIGVEDA
Dr. B. R. Kishore

Rigveda is the first and foremost of the Vedas. It underlines the path of Jnan or knowledge. It is hoped that this anthology of Rigvedic hymns would help a lot in the desired transformation and enlightenment of the readers.

144 Pages

ISBN 81-7182-020-4

YAJURVEDA
Dr. B. R. Kishore

Yajurveda is second of the four Vedas. It underlines the path of Karma or Action. It is a collection of sacred mantras or texts to be recited at the time of ritual sacrifice.

160 Pages

ISBN 81-7182-021-2

SAMVEDA
Dr. B. R. Kishore

Samveda underlines the path of Bhakti or Devotion. The hymns in this Veda are addressed to Indra, Soma & Agni. Among the four Vedas, it is regarded as the foremost. In Bhagvat Gita, Lord Krishna has declared, "Of the Vedas, I am Saman".

160 Pages

ISBN 81-7182-018-2

ATHARVAVEDA
Dr. B. R. Kishore

Atharvaveda Samhita, the fourth of the Vedas, is regarded to be the last. It deals chiefly with the practical side of life. It is concerned with man, his practical problems, protection from the enemy, politics and day-to-day welfare. It contains several hymns highly intellectual and philosophical in their contents and significance.

160 Pages

ISBN 81-7182-019-0

SRIMAD BHAGAVADGITA

Dayanand Verma

The Srimad Bhagavadgita is a part of the epic. "The Mahabharat". So, in order to assess the full import of the message given by the Gita, it would be better if we briefly recapitulate certain main events of Mahabharat.

This book would help the reader appreciate the cause behind Lord Krishna enlightening the gathering at Kurukshetra with his divine discourse called Shrimad Bhagavadgita.

186 Pages

ISBN 81-7182-067-0

MAHABHARATA

Dr. B. R. Kishore

The Mahabharata is an inclusive epic which deals with all possible human situations. It is an excellent book of Destiny, Doom and Dharma, all rolled together in one.

After going through the book, a sensible reader is bound to emerge a better person with greater strength of character and courage.

182 Pages

ISBN 81-7182-068-9

RAMAYANA

Dr. B. R. Kishore

The Ramayana is our first national epic. The reading of the book provides a great religious, literary and philosophical experience through which one would like to pass again and again.

176 Pages

ISBN 81-7182-070-0

HINDUISM

Dr. B. R. Kishore

The book presents the panoramic view of the popular Hinduism as well as its abiding and eternal principles, in a style simple and direct and yet lucid and vigorous.

192 Pages

ISBN 81-7182-073-5

QUIET TALKS WITH THE MASTER

Eva Bell Werber

It is an invaluable book for the spiritual upliftment of all people.

In moments of meditation these quiet talks were held with the Master of Men. They are sweet in Fellowship, simple in language, yet they contain truths as vital as have ever been given down the ages to man.

126 Pages

ISBN 81-7182-052-2

FUTURE IS IN OUR HANDS

A. Somasundaram

This invaluable book is a collection of the author's select spiritual writings in which he has forcefully presented a comprehensive vision of the New Era of Universal Peace, Love and Unity. It is full of remarkable insights into the future-building efforts by individuals and societies. This highly illuminating book will serve as precious treasure of functional spiritual ideas for the Humanity in the 21st Century.

It is a must for all enlightened people young and old, who are eager to have their bright future in this world and in the "Other World'.

234 Pages

ISBN 81-7182-164-2

ONENESS WITH GOD

Yogi Minocher K. Spencer

The book presents the essences of the different religions of the world and their teachings. It shows the various ways and means of God Realisation and superbly discusses the various paths that lead to the union with God.

The book is a must for all those who are really eager to gain spiritual knowledge and who crave for the dawn of the New Era of universal peace and love in the world.

234 Pages

ISBN 81-7182-054-9